FAMILY
by MARGARET MEAD
and KEN HEYMAN

FAMILY

by **MARGARET MEAD**
and **KEN HEYMAN**

A RIDGE PRESS BOOK

THE MACMILLAN COMPANY, NEW YORK

These became part of that child who went forth every day, and who now goes, and will always go forth every day.

— WALT WHITMAN

ACKNOWLEDGMENTS

Work on Bali appearing in this book was supported
in part by a grant from the National Institute of Mental Health, M-2118,
"Reconnaissance Recheck on Balinese Mental Health," 1957–1958.
The quotation on page 141 is from "There Was a Child
Went Forth," by Walt Whitman. The final words in the book are from
William Wordsworth's "Ode: Intimations of Immortality."

———————

The authors appreciate the photographic assistance of George W. Martin.
Ken Heyman is a member of Meridian Photographics.

EDITOR IN CHIEF: Jerry Mason
EDITOR: Adolph Suehsdorf
ART DIRECTOR: Albert Squillace
ASSOCIATE EDITOR: Evelyn Hannon
ASSOCIATE EDITOR: Ruth Birnkrant
ASSOCIATE EDITOR: Peter Lacey
ART ASSOCIATE: David Namias
ART PRODUCTION: Doris Mullane

Produced by The Ridge Press, Inc.
Published by The Macmillan Company, New York,
Collier-Macmillan Canada, Ltd., Toronto, Ontario.
Printed in the United States of America
by Western Printing and Lithographing Company.
Library of Congress Catalog Card Number 65-21158

CONTENTS

INTRODUCTION

This book has grown as a child grows. There was a period of long, slow growth before the book took shape. There were leaps and spurts as the book's own form began to emerge, anxiety and doubt as that form seemed to be changing, and the kind of reservations that parents also feel as they look in wonder at the person their child is becoming. As with a child whom a family must cherish, then slowly allow to become himself, and finally send out into the world to fend for himself, there comes a time when those who have cherished a new book must lay aside further hopes and dreams and let it go. What happens then depends on what other people make of it. Its future lies in other hands, in other hearts.

But the process of which this book is a part will go on. Elsewhere in the world Ken Heyman will find mothers who express their tenderness in other ways. Revisiting the South Sea children—long since become parents and grandparents—whom I studied twenty and thirty years ago, I shall find new understanding of the way their parents dried their tears and guided their faltering footsteps. Each time Ken Heyman returned home from one of the forty-five countries where he photographed the adults and children who are pictured here, his own small children greeted him with change, and these changes newly informed their father's perceptiveness. Similarly, the children I watched years ago, their children, and their children's children provide a living context for this book, which can only catch moments in time, however vividly, and hold them for the eyes of thousands.

The collaboration that led to this book has been a continually growing one. It had its beginning in 1954, in the relationship of teacher and student at Columbia University, when Ken, as part of his work, brought to my class photographs of the small slum children who had caught his imagination. It became a cooperative relationship in 1957, in Bali, where we went to photograph the children in villages I had studied twenty years before. There we worked side by side, as I selected the individuals and the scenes, and Ken literally and symbolically brought them into a new focus. Through the work we did during those hot, exhausting days, he learned what I was looking for and I learned what he could find in each scene. I learned what he could make of individuals, newly encountered, by following them intensively through an hour of living, and what caught his eye at the first glimpse of a seething crowd or a cluster of children playing by the corner of a deserted temple. I learned how closely he could move within a group and still leave its pattern undisturbed.

Two years later, in 1959, we went to a Mexican village, where we worked for five days among people who, although they were hospitable and kind, were total strangers. The record we made of this village was as anonymous as the Balinese record had been individualized and grounded in my old knowledge of the earlier lives of a particular group of people. This experience opened new possibilities. We began to see what could be done with photographs that can stand alone, without all the paraphernalia of detailed notes and genealogies that must underlie the photography that is part of a scientific record.

A single scene—a mother combing a child's hair, a father leading a child along a path, a child lonely beneath a wall, two sisters playing on the grass in a park—could be taken from the particular spatial and temporal context in which it was embedded, and a set of such pictures could be placed in the quite different context of their common humanity. Behind the single caught gesture there would always be the intricate social and political realities as well as the physical setting, the houses of stone or mud or straw, the affluence or the extreme poverty in which a whole people—or only some individuals—lived. Without diversity and contrast, commonalties of experience mean far less. But when each photograph is taken with a full recognition of the completeness of the whole pattern out of which the single scene is lifted and given pictorial permanence, the pattern itself remains as background. The differences among the families—the differences in the shape of their heads, the color of their skin, the brightness of their eyes, their stance and ways of moving, together with the differences in their surroundings and the kind of building each of them calls home—are a necessary but not a sufficient basis for what they have in common.

By placing side by side one hundred pictures of Bali, or by arranging in sequence a set of pictures showing the interplay among the members of a Mexican family, one can say something that could not otherwise be said about Bali or about Mexican personal relationships. In a parallel way we began to see the possibilities of grouping pictures from several countries so that the counterpoint would become significant. With this in mind, Ken Heyman prepared exhibitions that included photographs from two or more countries. In such an exhibit, the pictures taken in Bali, in the context of long knowledge, those taken in Mexico, in the context of brief, intensive association, those taken in the United States, as part of a long single exploration (as, for example, the photographs for his book, *Willie*), and those taken of strangers encountered by chance on new strange streets—all these formed one contrapuntally related whole.

This sense of wholeness is similar to the kind one occasionally comes on in a great collection of pottery. Each pot, shaped for some purpose by human hands, stands with other pots, also shaped by human hands, and the circumstance that half the earth's circumference and millenia in time separate the different makers is irrelevant. The common processes of pot making are explicit, and the eye that recognized how these shapes might be grouped together is implicit in their placement side by side. But there are certain limitations to such a collection of the work of human hands, or even a collection of paintings or carvings made by men at different periods or in different countries, that distinguish them from the exhibitions Ken Heyman prepared. For in a collection of pottery or paintings the one who makes the final choice, grouping the pots or hanging this picture where the light falls and that picture in shadow to point up the congruence of formal line or latent feeling, is bringing together finished objects, things completed long ago by men he never knew in lands whose villages and countryside evoke no memories of sight or sound or smell as he works. The objects brought together in the collection are torn genuinely out of context, and life must be breathed into them anew by the exhibitor and the spectators.

This book has a more pervasive wholeness. Every photograph was taken by the same person within a space of seven years—the earliest in 1957, the most recent only a few weeks before these words were written. The urgency of the heat and the smell of the streets and parks and newly mown fields is here. Noise and stillness, motion and relaxation are here. They entered into the experience of the photographer who carried to each new picture—in his own responsive movements, in the tautness of his hands holding the camera—the memories of the other faces he had seen, the other people among whom he had walked as a newcomer to whom every facet of their lives was expressive. These pictures are held together by a way of looking that has grown out of anthropology, a science in which all peoples, however contrasting in physique and culture, are seen as members of the same species, engaged in solving problems common to humanity.

In the past when a great religious story was taken from one people to another, those who heard it soon remodeled the saints from a faraway land, changing the settings in which they acted, their appearance, and even the color of their skin, to fit them into a local, more familiar picture of life. And as long as travelers had only words to describe all they had seen, listeners to travelers' tales could cast other peoples in their own image or picture them as monsters, different in kind from themselves. But this is no longer possible. Today's children, even children growing up in the most remote parts of the world, know something about the world's peoples as they actually are—different and not so different from themselves. For this they have the evidence of their own eyes.

In our contemporary world, no one can think or work with a single picture of what a family is. No one can fit all human behavior, all thought and feeling, into a single pattern. Just as the scope of our imagination has been enlarged by our awareness of orbiting satellites, and children now draw the earth with its green continents and blue seas within the larger setting of the solar system, so also our knowledge and experience have broken through the narrow provincialisms, the prejudices, and the naïvetes of the past and we are glimpsing new prospects. Flight at the speed of sound, telemetry that follows the pilot on his flight, and television that links the continents, all give us a sense of simultaneity that once was limited to a village street or the enclosed space of a courtyard, but now is world-encircling.

This immediacy of knowledge of the many kinds of people in the world, whose lives are full of contrast and yet are comparable, has informed Ken Heyman as he has traveled to one country and then to another. Within this framework, his sense of one country was not binding; instead, it directed his eyes in the next. All his pictures in this book have been taken since the launching of Sputnik, when we gained our new vision of a single world viewed from space. All of them were taken by a photographer who came to each place as an eager, interested stranger, with confidence in what his eye could see and with a special gift for entering without interrupting an on-going scene.

When he works within a family, however briefly, the very fact that he, a complete outsider, is permitted to witness the shared feast, the bathing of the child, the hours of relaxation when people have finished their day's work gives a special intimacy to his pictures—the intimacy that lifts a veil momentarily for the stranger, as the Mexican family did for us. Some of these interior scenes come from highly fortunate homes, others from homes of the very poor.

But most of the people, adults and children, photographed on the streets of strange cities, are poor. For it is prevailingly the poor of the world who gather on doorsteps, in parks, and on public beaches. They lack space indoors and have no gardens where their children can play safely under the trees. They lack walls to shut the stranger out of their lives.

In these photographs, the families who invited Ken into their homes give one a sense of private intimacy. The people thronging the streets, the children playing in the areaways and on the empty lots of slums, the fishermen, the vendors in the African markets, and the old women sitting against a wall in Portugal represent the restless millions of the earth, newly numerous in a world that has not yet found good places for them to live. Ken Heyman did not seek out the poor; they are everywhere.

This relationship of intimacy and public life is not accidental. All the things that have made this book what it is are interrelated: the high-speed film and the fast lenses used for the photography; the jet planes that made possible the rapid transitions from one country to another and the visits to remote peoples cut off for thousands of years from real contact with their fellows; the great political upheavals that have sent millions homeless into foreign lands and that have crowded other millions into homes that are only corners of single rooms; the discoveries of science that have resulted in a bursting of the dams that held the earth's populations in uneasy check, and those that now threaten the destruction of the human race; the scientific knowledge that we are all members of one species—a species that cannot rely on instinct, but must depend on what is learned and invented and can be passed on from one generation to another. This knowledge and our awareness of these relationships force us to recognize vast discrepancies in the lives of different individuals, in different sections of one country, and in different countries. These contrasts are intrinsic to the contemporary world, a world in which we are only beginning to realize our common humanity. And they are intrinsic to this book.

But when we search for forms of communication that will be intelligible everywhere and seek figures of speech that will be meaningful to all peoples, we can come back to the human body. When we search for common ways of expressing similarity and difference, hierarchy and equality, vulnerability and strength, we can look to the human body. And when we search for ways of describing human relationships—dependency, autonomy, trust, cooperation, or ecstasy—we turn almost inevitably to the family. For within the family we can trace the fine intricacy of living—in the cherishing character of parenthood, the contrasts between father and mother, the differences between children of like and of opposite sex, the chance that makes one brother stronger or one sister more beautiful than another, the ebb and flow of feeling, and the alteration of relationships as the child grows from infancy to adulthood and passes from his family of birth to found a family of his own.

As in our bodies we share our humanity, so also through the family we have a common heritage. This heritage provides us with a common language that survives and transcends all the differences in linguistic form, social organization, religious belief, and political ideology that divide men. And as men must now irrevocably perish or survive together, the task of each family is also the task of all humanity. This is to cherish the living, remember those who have gone before, and prepare for those who are not yet born.

MOTHERS

A mother accepts her child before she knows who that child will be.

As long as a mother is carrying her child, she cannot know its sex or the color of its eyes. She cannot know whether it will be strong and sturdy or weak and ailing, whether it will be a laughing baby or a sad and lonely one. Until it is born, she cannot know how intense its need of her will be or even whether it will live. She accepts on faith the child's coming into being and the child's identity, as yet unknown.

Motherhood begins with this willingness to accept the unknown. A mother knows whose the child is in the sense of who has begotten it, but she cannot know what its heritage may be from its long double line of ancestors. How her child, as yet unborn, will look five or ten or fifteen years hence can be known only when the time comes. Much is determined from the moment of conception—the child's hair color at birth and, in later years, its potential height, and the basic quality of its responses, quick or slow, outgoing or turned inward. The design of a person has been created, but it exists only as a promise, for the path from conception to birth is a hazardous one. Yet actual mishaps are becoming increasingly rare as modern medicine wards off many of the ancient dangers, and today people no longer expect difficulties to occur during pregnancy and childbirth, or fear that a child may die soon after it is born. Protective care has made us optimists.

Hundreds of thousands of years ago, human beings understood very little of the world they lived in. They were conscious and curious, but enormously ignorant of things we take for granted. They did not relate the presence and absence of the sun to the sequence of day and night. They did not know that plants grow from seeds. And we must assume that they did not understand the process of procreation. The connection between love-making and childbearing was an extraordinarily tenuous one. Even today, in some extremely isolated parts of the world, there are very primitive peoples who recognize that virgins do not bear children, but who do not have a physiological explanation of the child's coming into being. So also in the very distant past, early men, understanding very little about conception, built up the most varied beliefs about the child's origin, explanations that perhaps fitted the insistent reality of the quickening of life. The new child was a spirit for whom the man opened the way into the woman's womb. Or the new child was a long-departed ancestor who was once more returning to earth to hunt in the hills and fish in the streams. Later, as men came to understand more about themselves and other living beings, they recognized that both parents made a physical contribution to the child and built up new beliefs that incorporated this perception. The child received its bones from its father and its blood from its mother. Or the child received its blood from its mother and its soul from its father, a belief that stressed the mother's contribution. A very few peoples went to the other extreme of denying the mother any role but a caretaking one. The father deposited the new being in the woman's womb, where she sheltered it until it had grown to birth size. Still other peoples thought of the child as made of earth and believed that when the child was born, it would travel all its days toward the place whence that earth came until, dust from dust, to dust it would return. Even now, in spite of the great advances in man's scientific knowledge, vestiges of such beliefs live on in poetry, drama, folk sayings, and old wives' tales.

Women, and to a lesser extent men, have schooled their imagination in moments of wondering who a child will be, whom it will resemble, how its very first cry will sound, and who will evoke its first responding smile. Today some of these ancient questions have been reshaped by the tests that confirm a woman's pregnancy, the X-rays that determine the child's position, the stethoscope that reinforces the ear's listening for the foetal heartbeat, and, when the child is born, the careful measurements of weight and bone age that make it possible to judge how mature the newborn child is—whether it is still in need of a womb-like protection or is ready to confront the wind and weather of the outer world.

We have succeeded in analyzing away many uncertainties about the unborn child that amazed and frightened our primitive ancestors and that continue to amaze and frighten the peoples of the world who know nothing about science. But the essential mystery remains: *Who will the baby be?* Indeed, as we learn more about the intricate processes of inheritance, the mystery is not dispelled, but deepens with the recognition of the child's long heritage. It is the carrier not of the actual soul of a great-grandfather or great-grandmother, but of traits from ancestors far more remote in time. Each woman, knowing she is pregnant and knowing whose child she is carrying, must still be prepared, like her most primitive forebears, to cherish a being not yet known to her. And each woman is still left to ponder the mystery in her heart.

For most of human history the beginning of motherhood has been accompanied by danger. In the past a girl already knew, long before she herself was old enough to bear a child, of women who had died in labor and of infants who had failed to survive their birth. As surely as her brother grew up to know the dangers of manhood because he had seen men who had been mauled by wild beasts and knew of men who had never returned from sea voyages in small, unseaworthy boats, she herself grew up to recognize that her life of childbearing was hazardous. So clearly have some primitive peoples recognized this that they have treated as equal in bravery the woman who died in childbirth and the man who died in battle, and have seen in the rainbow's arch the bright shed blood of valiant fighters of both sexes.

The hazards of pregnancy and childbearing, like the mysteries of conception, have been a challenge to the imagination. Everywhere the expectant woman was enveloped in a protective cocoon of rules that defined what she must eat and not eat, what she must and must not do or say or see or think lest the child come to harm. She was forbidden to eat lively, quick animals; if she did, the child would be born too quickly. She was forbidden to use sharp instruments, since these might injure the child. She was forbidden to eat large or strangely shaped fruits; if she did so, this might prevent her child from growing into a normal human being. She had to be protected from frightening sights, for her fright could scar her child. And if she craved some special food—limes or sour plums—or the delicacy cooking in her neighbor's pot, she had to be given it at once; her unsatisfied cravings might endanger the child.

While the young mother listened to the old women and kept the taboos that protected the child's safety, the child grew and she cherished it in her imagination. Whether the old women told her she must continue to fetch firewood so that she would be strong enough to bear the child, or told her that she must not fetch firewood lest in breaking a branch she should break her child's bones, these acts of obedience and care bound her to her child and protected the child's future.

But many things were outside human control. Not knowing when a child would be born, the woman had no assurance that it would be born in a safe place. If her time came while the tribe, racing against sleet and snow, was driving the herds to their winter feeding grounds, people could not stop for the birth of a baby. The woman had to hope that the child would be born at night, so that by morning she could struggle to her feet and keep up with the rapid trek on which the lives of the whole group depended. Where women were the food gatherers, a pregnant woman could not refuse to do her share because she feared that her baby might be born while she was far from help. Wherever a people have lived on the edge of starvation and a woman's work has been essential to the life of the household, there has always been a conflict between the needs of the children already living and the needs of the unborn child.

All over the world today, wherever women must work daily in field or factory to earn money for their children's food, they are torn by some of the same fears that afflicted primitive women. Given neither time nor security, they know they are risking the child's life and their own, for when the child comes there may be no one who is ready to help them through the difficulties of labor and birth. Yet there is a fundamental difference. The primitive woman risked the life of her child for the welfare of the whole group and because there was no choice. In the contemporary world, the risk is a man-made one. Too often, as we conquer one kind of hazard, we introduce another. Today the well-nourished, well cared for, warmly loved woman can look forward to childbearing with far less trepidation and much greater hope than any woman could in the past. But she may be denied the simpler acceptance that her ancestors, so much more

15

ignorant and heavily burdened, could give the child growing within their bodies.

The moment of birth, dramatized in very different ways around the world, is not always seen as the moment of the child's full emergence on the human scene. There are peoples who treat the child's first days of life as a trial period during which the child will decide whether it finds its mother congenial and whether it wishes to remain in this world. Others are afraid to name the newborn child or to allow any outsider to gaze at it, lest some harm befall the child. And for thousands of years the infant who did not flourish on its mother's milk did not survive. But each mother and surviving infant formed a nursing couple, related to each other safely and rhythmically through the interdependence of the breast and milk of the mother and the mouth and growth of the child.

For the mother the task of childbearing was lightened and illuminated by the long months of infancy, while she fed her child who was now clearly identified, a boy or a girl, named and known, a person different from all others, a unique human being. Even very early civilizations played very differently on this central interdependence of mother and child. When a woman could not breast-feed her child, another woman sometimes took it into her care, and the hungry searching lips of the baby pressing on the adoptive mother's dry breasts filled them with milk to nourish the infant. In complex societies, women of rank have been freed from the task of feeding their own infants, and caste and class differences have been built on the contrast between the lady who bore a child and the wet nurse who nourished the lady's child at the expense of her own, because she was a poor relation, a commoner, a peasant, a slave, or a member of a subject race. This division between the mother who, by bearing a child, carried on the lineage on which rank and pride depended, and the nurse who, by suckling the child, created a lifelong bond with it had the indirect effect both of linking and of separating castle and cottage. For in later years men turned for comfort and love to women of lower rank. But the mothers who bore them still shaped their expectations about the kind of women who would bear their legitimate children and who would be the only suitable mates for their legitimate sons.

Wherever it has been customary for a mother to suckle her own infant, the child has been assured a continuing relationship with one human being who has satisfied its hunger and given it a sense of safety and trust. In the past, when the mother went any distance away from home, she had to carry her nursing infant with her, and when the child became too heavy to carry, she had to hurry home from the garden to feed it. Another woman might give it a little milk, or someone might feed it a soft mash of bananas or rice or taro. But the mother and the child could not be separated for long. Where people were poor or careless, so that children were left hungry and their needs were disregarded, these children in turn became grudging mothers who left their children hungry and comfortless for hours at a time and grudging husbands who disregarded the needs of their wives. For girls learn first at their mothers' breasts how to be mothers. And boys also learn from their mothers' care of them how they, as husbands, should care for their wives who are pregnant or feeding newborn children.

One effect of modern civilization has been to interrupt this ancient tie of early intimacy between a mother and her baby. For the mother now has a choice. In the past, birth—the physical separation of the child from the mother's body—meant the establishment of a new relationship between the mother and the child in her arms, the intensity of which was broken only with weaning to another kind of food. But today birth itself has become a form of weaning, as the modern mother chooses between distance and closeness to her child.

The feeding bottle opened the way to choice. Feeding her child from a bottle, a mother could modify the close interdependence of the nursing couple in the months during which the infant, carried in darkness as a stranger, discovered the nature of its welcome in the world. The feeding bottle made possible the establishment of total impersonality from the time of birth, and so an infancy without tenderness and warmth. But with the feeding bottle a mother also could keep alive the child who would not have thrived on her milk, and so it made possible warmth and tenderness between a mother and an infant who would otherwise have died.

With the feeding bottle came the carriage. The one made it possible for the mother to leave the baby; the other made it possible for her to take the baby with her. From the day when the baby carrier could be hung from the saddle of a horse down to the present, when the baby carrier can be strapped into the station wagon, inventions that have permitted the mother to journey abroad accompanied by her child have competed with inventions that have permitted her to leave it behind. Both kinds of invention have lessened her immediate physical contribution to her child's upbringing. Mixing a formula neither alters her figure nor strains her body. Pushing a high-wheeled baby carriage does not strain the muscles of her back and arms. But both increase the distance between the mother and the child, each of whom loses in part the continual reinforcement of bodily contact, the mutual adaptation, and the slowly growing realization that each of them is a separate entity. By introducing greater flexibility, both kinds of invention have opened the way to wider choice. Both have made choice a necessity.

The process of civilization, while it has lightened the woman's physical load, has in many ways made motherhood a harder rather than an easier task. A woman can choose whether or not she will marry and whether or not she will bear a child, two choices that were not open to her primitive forebears. A woman who lacks the capacity to breast-feed her infant, or who chooses not to do so, still can give it adequate nourishment. She can keep her child warm and safe without cradling it against her body. Where her own knowledge is deficient, she can turn to others—not the old women who were the carriers of tradition, but scientifically trained specialists in the care of children—who can help her to interpret the needs of each small, unique human being. All these things lighten the burden of motherhood and open the way to greater security for more children.

But society also can construct situations that introduce new hazards. Social arrangements may exist in which illegitimate children are born whom no one is prepared to care for and cherish. A style of marriage may become fashionable in which parenthood begins very early and children follow one another in close succession. In a marriage of this kind the young mother may become so frantic and destructive that she may turn against her young children whom she cannot love and care for as she knows she should. Or a very young mother may be left alone to rear her child with only an impersonal clinic and a welfare worker to help her create a safe and human setting and to keep alive some link of communication with the world. Or a mother may be forced to put her child into strangers' hands while she goes out to work. Modern civilization has made it possible for almost every baby to live and almost every mother to care for her child, but it also has created new dilemmas. Modern women are freed from the terrors of the unknown, the dangers of giving birth in the dark and the cold, the anxieties of meeting an infant's need for food—the worst difficulties that haunted the imagination of primitive women. But civilization confronts us with difficulties of our own making and sets new conditions for motherhood.

Yet the modern mother still is asked to love her child unconditionally, and the child now, as in the past, is dependent on her unconditional love. The child who has experienced safety, warmth, and comfort in its mother's arms carries with it a sense of personal worth and of trust in human relationships that makes tolerable the tasks and difficulties that must be faced later in life. The child whose mother has succeeded in giving it a sense of being valued as a unique individual, entirely for itself, without regard for the accidents of beauty or brains or special talent, is prepared as a person to meet the challenges of living. We do not know—man has never known—how else to give a human being a sense of selfhood and identity, a sense of the worth of the world, and an abiding trust in human relationships. Without these, growing up is very hard, and sometimes may be impossible.

As we find ways of supplementing the mother's single, often frail and insufficient body, and of making more flexible the bonds between mother and child, we are also making the discovery that there is no substitute for the mothering relationship. For this reason, in spite of all the changes that have been introduced by modern inventions, the model for motherhood remains what it has always been—the relationship between the mother's body and the body of her child. The womb, the gates of life, the child's first breath and gasping cry, the first moment at the breast, the warmth of the mother's cradling arms, the rhythms of feeding and holding, sleeping, waking, reaching out, and slipping into quiet, in which mother and child are partners—all these are part of mothering. And the central image of the mother's physical care and love for a small human being who has been and continues to be wholly dependent on her for its life and health carries with it the proviso of the mother's absolute acceptance of her child. Faced by a child who cannot thrive on her love, a mother is helpless. But the love and care a child evokes in its mother does not depend on whether it is beautiful or homely, plump or thin, fretful or content; as long as it lives—and, hopefully, thrives—it is hers to care for. It is this absolute, unconditional acceptance that every child needs. Lacking it, a human being never ceases to seek it.

During the long months of infancy, while the child's tie to the mother is a bodily one, the child learns through its own body what the world is like and what it is to be a person. As the mother feeds the child when it is hungry, the child learns that the world can be trusted to provide the things it needs. As the mother senses her child's sleepiness and lulls it to sleep, the child learns to fit together feeling and action and is given a first sense of appropriateness. As the mother smiles when her child smiles, pouts when it pouts, and smacks her lips or clucks in response to its first playful babbling, the child learns that the world is a place in which people can reciprocate moods and meaning.

Each new learning is a new delight for the mother whose attention is focused so closely on the child that its slightest gain is manifest and significant of its lively growth and awareness. As a mother learns to respond to the restless rootling of her hungry baby, to its breaking smile or puckered frown, to its look of recognition, and to its first puzzled attempt to put sound and meaning together, she reinvokes her own infancy, when she could elicit a quick responsiveness at her mother's breast. As she was once the child who reached toward a mother who was only dimly perceived and understood, now she can be, at the same time, mother and child. For a woman, motherhood rounds the circle in which her own childhood is given back to her in all its satisfying delight.

As a little girl she learned to follow her mother's eyes as they moved over the faces of the other members of the family, watchful for the slightest shadowing of anxiety or fear, weariness or hunger. Now she experiences in full measure how her mother learned to practice this watchfulness, as she herself looks solicitously at her child, quick to catch the first shiver of cold, the first attempt to practice some new learning—the hand reaching out gingerly to touch and meeting its object with a new precision, the foot set more firmly on the floor. From this watchfulness of the baby who has not yet learned to talk, she is drawn into an awareness of the child's emerging thinking, and recognizes the abstractions that underlie a single word that means good and food and grandma, or glass and window and diamond. As her child's mind rushes out to grasp the world around it, she moves with it over a remembered path, her imagination no longer bound by adult conventions, but dancing freely in step with the child.

Later the mother must wean her child, breaking the physical bond in such a way that as the child takes a first step away from her into the world, she herself can once more become a whole and separate person. Weaning, both in the literal sense of weaning from the breast or the bottle and in the figurative sense of weaning from the mother's constant presence and helping hand, is successful if it gives the child the confidence to use the love and security it has been given.

Every act of motherhood contains a dual intent, as the mother holds the child close and prepares it to move away from her, as she supports the child and stands it firmly on its own feet, and as she guards it against danger and sends it out across the yard, down by the stream, and across the traffic-crowded highway. Unless a mother can do both—gather her child close and turn her child out toward the world—she will fail in her purpose. And often, as a mother bathes, feeds, and dresses her child, her face expresses two kinds of feeling that seem contradictory to the child and to the bystander. There is the look of unconditional devotion and blind pride in this, her child, and at the same time a look of anxious appraisal as she holds the infant away from her breast or watches the toddler's first stumbling steps and rocking gait.

For the child must go forth from the warmth and safety of its mother's care—first to take a few steps across the room, then to join playmates, and later to go to school, to work, to experience courtship and marriage, and to establish a new home. A boy must learn how different he is from his mother; he must learn that his life is turned outward to the world. A girl must learn, as she walks beside her mother, that she is both like her mother and a person in her own right. It is one of the basic complications of a mother's life that she must teach one thing to her sons and other things to her daughters.

Some peoples emphasize the mother's task more than the child's; they say that it is the mother, not the child, who is weaned. But all peoples, however differently they phrase the mystery of conception and provide for the care and safety of the mother and the child at birth, make provision—some well and others in a blundering way—for this double aspect of motherhood. All peoples build into their conception of the relationship of mother and child the care that must continue and the slowly awakening recognition that these are two persons—at birth, at physical weaning, at the child's first step, and at the child's first word that allows the child to call from a distance. And as the child lets go of its mother's hand, sure that it can return to be fed and rocked and comforted, the father, whose tie to the child is so much less physical, reaches out his hand. As another person, he helps the child to establish its own sense of identity as a member of society, always further removed from infancy at its mother's breast.

In the small family, the child has only a mother and a father and perhaps a brother or sister, close in age, to fill out its world. Where there are no other women in the home, the mother has to be all things to the child, and any shift in her attention, any weariness, is immediately reflected in the exchange of mood between child and mother. But the child who grows up in a large household learns to trust many kinds of people. Moving among many brothers and sisters or within a large circle of aunts, uncles, cousins, and grandparents, the child learns to differentiate among them. One is heavy-handed and another has a light and delicate touch, one has the gift of laughter and another is a sure refuge in moments of trouble, one gives a quick hug and another a cookie. But through it all, the child needs the continuity of care given by its mother (or the nurse who takes her place) as the one person who can respond to each small change in mood, who feels the fret and tension that come before a fever, who knows the new tooth is coming before it shows, who recognizes a word as it emerges from babble. On this unbroken continuity, on this ebb and flow of feeling between the child and the mothering woman, depends the child's sense of being a whole, continuing person—the same person today, yesterday, and tomorrow, the same person tired or rested, hungry or satiated, sleepy or wakeful, adventurous or quietly contented.

The woman who tenderly mothers a child and endows it with the strength and will to grow need not be the one to whom the child was born, but when she is, it is easier for both of them. The biological mother is deeply committed to her child before it is born and builds on this first commitment. The mother who cannot build on the physical tie of pregnancy and consciousness at the moment of birth, who has not fed the child at her breast and rocked it to sleep in her arms, must depend on greater awareness and a disciplined watchfulness instead of the less conscious watchfulness that grows as the child grows. Her awareness of herself and her awareness of the child must round the circle in a different way.

Yet, in spite of the long months of physical intimacy, each mother taking her new-born child into her arms welcomes a stranger. Today this may be doubly so. In the past, the infant whose hereditary rhythms were too different from its mother's could not thrive, and died. For thousands of years other women looked on helplessly as mothers died in childbirth and as the newborn failed to respond to life. But today almost all women live to welcome their babies, and almost every child that is born can live. And among the children who are born and live, there are some who are veritable strangers, for some survive with handicaps that require an extraordinary display of maternal love and imagination, and some with gifts set in such fragile bodies that no one like them could have survived in the past. New knowledge implements our hope and challenges each mother of a child to a new fulfillment of her task of welcoming a human being.

IRAN

JAPAN

GHANA

U.S.A.

23

DENMARK

VENEZUELA

U.S.A.

U.S.A.

POST NO BILLS

OST NO BILLS

NO BALL PLAYING

▼ FRANCE

32

GREEC

34

BRAZIL ▼ KENYA

U.S.A.

PANAMA

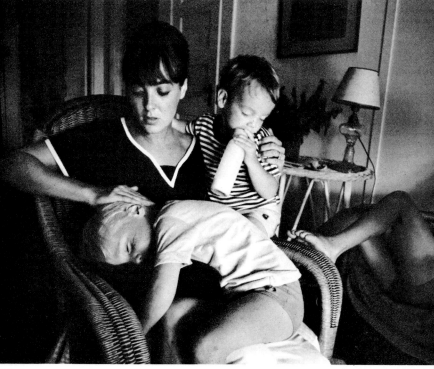

U.S.A.

PERU

GERMANY

ITALY

TURKEY

DENMARK

FATHERS

Children grow toward their fathers.

The moment of birth is a moment of separation, and all through infancy the child becomes more of an individual in its own right, less a part of the mother and less dependent on her constant care. From the moment of birth the child grows toward the father, and the father learns to accept this small creature with flailing arms and legs as his own. The child's tie to its mother is a deeply biological one that human beings share with all mammals that protect the growth of the very young organism within the mother's body. But the child's tie to its father is a social one that links these two from the day of the child's birth when, as it is phrased in some societies, the father "recognizes" this child as his. For the father who shares actively in the care of an infant—plays with it, bathes it, carries it outdoors in his arms—this becomes a very strong bond, an insistent reason for hurrying home from the fields, from hunting or fishing, from a factory or an office. As he turns in from the road and as he enters the door, he listens for the sounds that tell him all is well.

Even the most primitive peoples, although they may have no knowledge of the role men play in procreation, insist that women must have husbands, so that children may have fathers. Every people believes that there must be at least one grown man who will care for the mother, provide shelter and food, guard and teach the child, and give it a stable place in the world. There are no people anywhere, whatever their race and however simple and primitive their way of life, who do not have the idea of legitimacy; there are no people who do not, in the simplest sense, differentiate between a child with a recognized father and a child without one.

But there is great variation in the treatment of the child born out of wedlock. Some peoples do not allow the fatherless child to live. Others give over responsibility for the illegitimate child and its mother to the men of the mother's family, that is, to her father

45

or brothers. Still other societies relegate such children to the care of strangers in an impersonal institution; and there these children without identity, whose guardians represent neither father nor mother, waste away and often die, even though they may be cared for under the most hygienic conditions. Without a recognized father, whether he is living or dead and whether he is the child's biological father or another man who stands in his place, the child has no social existence.

As long as procreation was not understood, the tie between a man and his child was established through the events of day-by-day living. A man chose his mate, or a mate was chosen for him. She might be a young girl or a woman who already had children. But she was recognized as his to protect, and children as they were born became part of the home, a recognized extension of the relationship between the man and the woman. Home was some kind of enclosed, protected, and private place—a cave, a brush lean-to, a tree house, a hearth, or a hammock swung between other hammocks in a communal house. There a man lived with the woman who was his wife—sometimes with more than one woman—and the children belonging to the household. A very small place was made for the newborn child, and if it died only a very small niche was left vacant. Some peoples counted it unlucky to assume that the small stranger would certainly stay. Very pointedly they made no advance preparations for its coming, and if it departed no single article of clothing, or even a mat bed, marked its brief tenancy.

But as a child grew in strength, it was given a name, perhaps many names. Instead of calling it "mouse" or "caterpillar," or some other derogatory term, in the hope of deflecting the attention of evil spirits, parents felt it safe to acknowledge the child's humanity and to adorn or ornament it as a boy or a girl. With this, the father's tie to the child, so intangible at birth, was made more explicit. For now he could carry his child out of the house and into the village to show it off, carry it home when his hunting was done, relieving his wife who still had nuts or berries to gather, or even carry it on a longer trip cradled comfortably on his shield. As it became more certain that this child, his child, would live and grow and someday become a man or a woman, the bond between father and child also became stronger.

Long before the parents' actual part in creating a child was known, people undoubtedly had preferences that were expressed in the hope that the unborn child would be a boy (or a girl), a hope that grew more insistent when one child after another of the same sex was born. There are peoples who prefer boys to girls and also those who prefer girls to boys. In spite of such preferences, all peoples do realize that some kind of balance between the sexes must be maintained to keep a society going.

Everywhere, after making sure that the newborn child is intact and breathing, the midwife or doctor looks for the child's sex and may announce, "Look at your son!" or "Here is your daughter!" Then, depending on the society into which the child is born, the onlookers may think, "Our people will be ruled by a queen!" or, "Perhaps he will be a great priest!" Or the father may exclaim, "Perhaps she will be a dancer like her mother!" or, "Ah, a wonderchild!" or, "Someday he may be president!" Or more simply, the image of a girl in her floating bridal veil or of a boy swinging a baseball bat may drift through the mind of one parent or the other. Throughout the ages people have prayed and made offerings, have followed old wives' prescriptions, and have made magic in the hope of bringing some influence to bear on the sex of the unborn child. But in the end, almost all children are accepted for what they are. With joy or resignation, parents say, "Male and female created he them."

Naming is one of the ways of asserting a father's relationship to his child. Since very early times men have passed on to their children names they themselves have received from their fathers, or, alternatively, a man gave his sister's child a name he had received from his mother's brother. Names, rights, privileges—the right to hunt in a territory or to fish a length of stream, the right to tell a story, sing a song, or dance a special dance, the right to wear a war charm or use a certain hunting magic, the right to practice a craft or to belong to a guild, the right to erect one's house in a certain place—all were rights that were owned and passed on from one generation to the next. Passed on to children or to sisters' children, rights and privileges such as these helped to establish each child's place in society and underlined the responsibility men took for their children and for succeeding generations long after they themselves were dead.

Although no one knows how the facts of physical procreation came to be known, we can safely assume that women must have worked out the connection between intercourse and pregnancy and must have learned to count the days and moons that established the identity of the fathers of their children. Yet long after the facts were known, many peoples continued to treat them as if they were irrelevant, and children were claimed by men who could not have begotten them. Nevertheless, distinctions based on physical heredity were made. People marked the individual differences among a group of children, noted the likeness to father or mother or some more remote ancestor, and recognized the recurrence of particular traits. With the recognition of physical resemblances to both parents went the idea that skin color or the shape of the nose, special abilities and emotional traits—an ear for music, a quick temper—could be inherited from either the mother or the father and might reappear in children of either sex, generation after generation.

But these possibilities of inheritance were reinterpreted in different ways. Among some peoples, the father's contribution to his child is regarded as all-important; the mother only shelters the new life, treating the unborn child like an honored guest. Then the important tie between mother and child may be the milk tie, a tie that can also be established with a foster mother who has suckled the child at her breast. In many societies the father is given complete rights over his children, and he will permit them to remain with an estranged wife only so long as they are very young and need her constant attention. The father's biological claim to a child is the weaker one, for while it can be proved scientifically that a man is not the father of a child, it cannot be proved that he is the father of a given child. However, in those countries where women and children take the man's name, law and custom may make his the stronger claim.

Once the biological facts were known, the tie of intimacy between father and child based on his day-by-day care could, and often did, disappear. In more complex societies, where men occupied high-ranking or specialized positions as chiefs, kings, and noblemen, statesmen and bankers, doctors and artists and scholars, they had the means of commanding the services of subordinates, relatives, servants, or slaves. When this happened, an ever-widening distance separated a man from his heirs. A host of woman servants, slaves, or occasionally eunuchs looked after infants and children in an important household. And although a man might anxiously await the birth of an heir and exercise the most exacting supervision over his children's care and education, he himself might have almost no personal contact with them. Beautifully bathed and dressed, meticulously trained in courtesy, the royal child might be brought into the father's presence once a day, once a week, or even less frequently—and that was all. Only very recently, in some countries, has intimacy been restored as eminent men—men whose power and prestige set them apart from their countrymen—take time to know their children and take part in their physical care.

Knowledge of physical paternity also made it possible for a man to absent himself from home for years or even decades. Once a man had safely begotten a child, he could sail away to fight or work and live in a foreign land; on his return, he could claim the child, now grown to manhood or womanhood, as his, not by virtue of day-by-day association and care, but merely because he had performed the procreative act.

Law and custom define the formal relationship of father and child, and day-by-day association creates a bond of intimacy. But the recognition of biological paternity has made possible distant fathers, disinterested fathers, absentee fathers, demanding fathers, and fathers who without lifting a hand to help a child may be exigent and relentless in their demands. The belief that a child is indeed his child, bone of his bone and flesh of his flesh, has made it possible for a man to take inordinate pride in his children, especially his sons, and also to feel deep humiliation in their failure to measure up to his high expectations. And awaiting the birth of a child, a man can take an active interest in his wife's pregnancy and interpret it as their pregnancy rather than hers alone. Sympathetic biochemical changes may occur in his body also, and as men did among some primitive peoples, he may share in the work of childbirth, sustaining his wife and welcoming their child at the moment of birth.

Through the ages, people have elaborated on the relationship between children and personal immortality. One of civilization's recurrent themes is built on this idea, which, taking many forms, may place on the child the responsibility of laying his father's restless ghost, tending his father's shrine, carrying on his father's name, ruling where once his father ruled, or over a longer span, re-embodying an ancestor. Continuities of this kind are challenged, revised, and rejected, only to be renewed in some other form. The desire to live on in the child, especially the male child, the hope of seeing one's own youth re-enacted, the belief that in one's old age the child will be an emblem of one's early vigor and promise and accomplishments, the wish that the child will carry on the unfinished business of one's life—these emotions are related to a dream that is so congenial to human beings that it triumphs over every rule against individual social inheritance, every attempt to equalize the lives of all men.

This emphasis on lineage differentiates a father's feeling for his son and for his daughter. A man without a son may turn to his daughter, or through his daughter to his son-in-law or his grandson, to carry on his name, his craft, or his dynasty. But they are only substitutes for the thing he lacks. The father's desire for immortality, whatever form it may take, is essentially embodied in his son.

In the United States, perhaps more than in any other country, we have sought to curb this desire of the father to perpetuate himself in his son. We legislate against nepotism. We actively discourage the father's daydream that his son will succeed him in his occupation or profession—that he will stay on the farm, become a doctor, or go into the family business—through our articulate expectation that a son will go further than his father did. This denial of a deeply rooted desire has had the effect, in contemporary American life, of focusing attention on the earliest years of a boy's relationship to his father. In the United States the image of a son is mainly that of a little boy, and a father expects his sons to grow away from him as they become adults. With this expectation the father cherishes his sons' early years and grudges whatever days, weeks, months, or years he may have to spend out of contact with them while they are still growing up.

Nevertheless, whether a father spends many hours with his children or sees them very seldom and only in the most formal contexts, he stands in contrast to the mother from the very start of his children's life. Whatever the nature of his particular relationship to his sons and daughters, he provides the dynamic contrast that makes it possible for them to grow up and in their turn beget or bear children, adults in an adult world.

For the very small baby, the father is the embodiment of strength. Unless the father is an old, decrepit man or still just a boy, unless he is a cripple or exceptionally frail, he is stronger than the mother. Once accustomed to handling a baby, he holds it with a firm, proud ease that gives the child a sense of being in contact with power, a kind of power that must be respected and can be trusted and enjoyed. Your father can let you stand on his stomach, he can lift you high in the air, toss you up and catch you safely in his strong arms. Whereas a mother's touch is compounded of tenderness and care, a father who is sure of himself can play the game with a fine abandon. But this very abandon can be frightening, too. A father's hands not only are larger and stronger than a mother's, they are also harder and rougher. Without losing its responsiveness to its mother's soft skin, the child must develop a capacity for trusting and enjoying a touch that is harsher and rougher, a body that is much more responsive to the excitement of risks.

For the very small child, its mother is a refuge. Head leaning in toward her breast, head hidden in her lap, whole body screened by her skirt, the child takes refuge with its mother and feels protected from anything or anyone strange, threatening, or hateful in the world, including its father. Father, even for the very small child, represents the outside world. He comes home from the outside in the evening and in the early morning he vanishes again. In contrast, the mother is always there—or almost always. When she goes away, the child protests, cries and screams, clings and tries to force her to stay. But the child learns to wait for the father. "When will you come?" "How long can you stay?" "When will you go away?" "Where are you going?" And finally, "Take me with you" out in the boat, up on the horse, out in the car, up in the plane.

As the first representative of the outside world, the father also can be unpredictable, startling, even frightening. The risks of playing with father can be breathtaking, and a game played with him can turn into a game of playing with fear. The father who still keeps a sense of his child's small body can give his son a sense of triumph that stands him in good stead all his life. But the father who rubs his unshaven cheek too hard against the child's, the father who tosses the child higher and higher, not noticing how the first screams of delight have changed to screams of pure terror, robs him of the ability to take the risks on which a boy tries out his maleness and on which many of the tasks of manhood depend.

49

Together with his strength and love of risks, his ability to push the game to the limits of the child's strength and his own, there is the fact that father seems so very big. When his father is away, a child forgets how tall he is, how loud his voice is, and what a boom goes through the whole house when he blows his nose or bursts into a roar of laughter. A father is so tall that when a small child looks up at him, what he sees is a pair of hairy nostrils—an image that is so frightening that few adults can recall the actual sight. But the fear lives on in children's stories of giants and the puny boys who challenge their disproportionate might.

Because father is tall, the little child lifted to his shoulder to look out at the world can see more than the taller children who must watch from the ground. Raised above the eye level of the tallest man, the child feels his own sense of himself expand. Around the world, children argue as to whose father is the tallest, the strongest, the most important of them all. Children can take their failures to their mothers, in whose care they can regain composure and strength; they depend on their fathers to urge them on to success.

For the small boy there comes a time when he senses himself to be almost a man, with a man's definite desires and passions. But in spite of his new consciousness, he must pause and settle down to the long years during which he will have to make his peace with the tall, strong man who tells him, "Wait, wait, you are not grown yet! Wait, learn, practice, go to school. Someday you will be a navigator; someday you will drive a car. Someday, many years from now, you will be a man. Don't try to act like one too soon. Wait, but be manly." As long as his son was a tiny child, the father could spend his tenderness freely in their play. Later, when his son is older, the father only half remembers his own struggle to be brave and strong and yet wait, his angry unwillingness to give up competition with grown men and go on being a child, learning and waiting for full manhood.

Yet this is a battle he must have fought. Otherwise he would not now be an adult with a wife and a child, a home and a means of livelihood. The battle may have been a very hard-fought one and his victory a feather's weight removed from defeat. He may just have managed to go out and face the other boys when his father called him a coward and put a chip on his shoulder. He may just have succeeded in choking back the bitter, furious words that he longed to hurl at his father, a grown man who commanded him to be brave as a man while he was still a child.

Now when his own son has reached the age at which he sometimes lost out and sometimes won, memories of these earlier occasions come back, half-memories shifting like the patterns of a kaleidoscope. And the child in front of him, on the edge of tears, desperate, frightened, pleading to be let off from the errand in the dark, the trip over the reef, the stream crossing where the crocodiles are, the walk up the block where the bigger boys are bullies who loom over him, the Little League game in which he knows he cannot catch a fast ball—the whole scene with its threat of defeat is inextricably mixed with his own memories. But after all he gritted his teeth and met the challenge. If he had not forced himself, he would not be here now, a man with a son. And gritting his teeth again, he makes the same unyielding demands that he once made on himself, and his son, frightened and sullen, goes out to meet the challenge in his turn. The more confident a father is of his own strength and his own success as a man and the milder his own struggle was to become a man, the more mild and confident he can be with his own son. Yet even the father for whom the struggle was a gentle one knows that it was necessary and that he must challenge his sons as once he was challenged, so that they will not merely wait but also become men.

During transitional periods of great change, fathers often lose their sense of certainty. Men are asked to give up hunting and instead to herd cows or sheep; they are asked to give up a roving life and instead to till the soil—in their eyes, women's work. They are forced to give up a kind of life that allowed them to plan their own work and when they would do it. Instead, they must now take a job under a boss on an assembly line. Or they emigrate to a country where they have neither the language nor the skill to be the men their fathers taught them to be. Confused and perplexed, such men may hand their sons over to women, and the women must urge little boys to be rough and tough and strong, admonishing where they cannot set a model and attempting both to comfort and to challenge their sons. It is far simpler for the son when the father, proud of what he can do and sure enough of himself to have patience, can set his son's feet on the ground and direct him toward goals both of them can understand.

In most parts of the world, the boy learns what men do from his father, learning with his muscles and his eyes long before he can pull on an oar, play a violin, drive a car, or draw a straight line on a drawing board. Watching a father perform some part of his work that is visible and dramatic is something millions of city children are robbed of, except during a few precious weeks of vacation when, if they are lucky, they can see their father doing things he does well. Elsewhere, children learn only a little from their father before they are sent away to learn from strangers in another valley, at court, as apprentices, or in school. In still other places the child has many teachers from the beginning. There the father's task may be a simpler one—to be indulgent while his wife's brother does the disciplining; to be understanding, because someone else does the punishing; to be firm and tough, because someone else will dry the child's tears.

But today, as the size of the family is diminished and as more of the world's peoples live in the small family of father, mother, and children, the father's importance as a model for the son and as a link to the outside world for all the children is intensified. He must teach his child how to win and how to lose, how to want to grow up and how to be patient with his small size and lack of skill, how to grit his teeth when he would rather give up, and how to take the next rung on the ladder. Often there are no uncles to share his task nor any male teachers in the classes for little children. Carrying a greater responsibility than any other father, the modern, city-dwelling father must himself do all the things that should be done by men for small boys.

Whatever a father's relationship may be with his daughter, it is never quite the same as with his son. For just as a boy very soon realizes that he and his father are males, the little girl realizes very early that her father is different from herself. She can lean back on her mother, knowing that one day she too will be a woman; with her father she must reckon quite differently. She sees her father come in from and go out into the world beyond the home. But where, for her brother, this is a world that he will someday enter, for her it is an alien place from which invaders may come into her home. And where her brother learns from his father's strong, rough hands that he must be brave and not cry out, the little girl must learn to trust, even though she is frightened, and when she is older she must find out how to convey gently and subtly that his hands were too rough that he tossed her too high, that she doesn't want him to do it again. A father who was more than usually timid and was teased about his girlish traits may be hard on his daughter, punishing in her the weakness he feared in himself. Or he may be unable to treat a girl differently from a boy and force all kinds of inappropriate skills on her. Or he may react by keeping her from the games and play he permits her brothers. He may, in fact, treat his daughter as another part of himself and yet as a being who cannot carry on his name or insure his immortality in some other way.

A father may emphasize his daughter's femininity more than her childishness and in doing so he may treat her with the gallantry or the importunity that characterizes his relationship with a grown woman. Even as he curbs and tames and mocks his son's springing sexuality, he may encourage his daughter to posture and flirt with him as one day she will with a suitor. Or he may coax out his daughter's charm, a charm that will make her irresistible to other men. Treated with a mixture of gentle roughhouse and undemanding and unthreatening solicitude, and discovering that she is cherished because she is a girl, a daughter can learn to trust herself with men and to expect that men will be strong and protective in their care for her.

In those societies in which the contrast between men and women is heavily empha-sized, a father may leave his daughter with her mother and her grandmother, treating her from birth as a being who lives in a different world from his, a being to whom the world of men and men's affairs is forever closed. Such a little girl must learn who she is from her mother and the other women around her. From her father she learns only that she is a stranger to him and that when she grows up she will be no less alien to other men.

There are also societies in which the father cultivates certain qualities in his children of both sexes and leaves other qualities to be cultivated by the mother. The father may deal with the outside world—teach his sons and daughters to walk, paddle or punt a boat, swim, climb mountains, read the newspapers or a map, take a journey, and meet strangers. At the same time their mother may teach them to be mannerly and quiet, orderly and careful in their tasks, attentive to those who make demands on them. Or it may be the father who is the disciplinarian, and the mother who is indulgent with all the children.

Either sex can take on any of these tasks, but however they are done the funda-mentals remain. In rearing a son, the father is rearing someone who is basically like himself; in rearing a daughter, he is rearing someone who is basically different. When a girl resembles her father in physique, brains, or courage more than her brothers do, he may be tempted to equate sex with temperament and bring up his daughter to feel she is a failure because she is not a boy. When a boy has the physique or the disposition that attracted his father to his mother, he may be led astray by these characteristics that cross sex lines and treat his son as if he were not fully a male.

Every society stylizes the way a father treats his children from infancy to adulthood. But no society has devised a foolproof system within which all men and women become equally felicitous and satisfactory parents for all their children. But since public life is principally in the hands of men, the continuity of civilization rests on the way fathers in each generation prepare their sons and their daughters to be the men and the women who will carry it on.

INDONESIA ▼ U.S.A.

GHANA

HONG KONG

59

U.S.A.

RANCE

INDIA

SWEDEN

FRANCE

PERU

65

INDIA

PORTU

EL SALVADOR

NIGERIA

U.S.S.R.

SWITZERLAND

DENMARK

70

U.S.A.

FRANCE

71

IRELAND

U.S.A.

NEW ZEALAND　　U.S.A. ▲

U.S.A.

FAMILIES

As far back as our knowledge takes us, human beings have lived in families. We know of no period when this was not so. We know of no people who have succeeded for long in dissolving the family or displacing it. Instead, men have exercised their imagination in the elaboration of different styles of family living and different ways of relating the family to the larger community.

A family may consist only of parents and children, and its fragile stability may rest on the simple personal choice of a man and a woman to stay together. Or a family may extend in time through all the remembered generations of ancestors and all the expected generations of children to come. Each family may see itself as a small independent unit, set apart and living in privacy behind closed doors. Or a sense of family may permeate a whole community, all of whose members count themselves kin. Or through a far scattered kindred the sense of family may extend throughout a country, so that a man can travel hundreds or thousands of miles, always with the expectation of arriving at a home and finding people to whom he feels related.

In the distant past, as men organized more complex societies, invented rank and class and caste, conquered other men and took slaves, built up cities, and traveled the great rivers and the high seas to meet and mingle with peoples who were very different from themselves, countless variations on the family theme developed. A man might have several wives, but unless some catastrophe decimated a generation of men, only a few could have many wives, for otherwise some men went wifeless. Or the old men might appropriate all the young women. Occasionally, in a few societies, one woman might share several husbands. Occasionally, under very rigid forms of state rule, marriage was tightly controlled. There large numbers of women might be cloistered and forbidden to marry; large numbers of men might be chosen to serve for years in the army; children might be taken from their parents to be reared in public nurseries. At different times there have also been small utopian societies in which property was held in common and the special ties between particular parents and children were minimized. Such solutions as these have been attempted by many peoples in many parts of the world. Within our own lifetime, special versions were put into practice in Russia, in the earlier days of the Soviet Union, and in the kibbutzim in Israel, as the first settlers worked to make the desert bloom. A new version is being tried out now in the People's Republic of China. Plato, in the *Republic,* developed a ground plan for an ideal society; the Incas of Peru, in their short-lived empire, attempted to create a state-controlled society. But so far, wherever they have been put into practice, such plans have failed in their ultimate purpose. The great harem and the state. nursery have survived only briefly during a period of autocratic rule or in a time of planned social change. Again and again, in spite of proposals for change and actual experiments, human societies have reaffirmed their dependence on the family as the basic unit of human living—the family of father, mother, and children.

No society has asked women to bear and rear their children alone or to provide for their children's shelter and food without the cooperation of at least one adult man. Occasionally the emphasis may shift. A man may do more for his sister's children or his daughter's children than he does for his own, but he is not cut off from his children; he only has a more limited responsibility for them. Occasionally, as in the contemporary world, in societies that so often fail in the task of bringing up men and women who can maintain stable families, the state may have to substitute for absent fathers. Instead of the father bringing home money for food and rent, a welfare check comes through the mail, and the mother, as lonely as her widowed forebears ever were, must carry on alone.

However, even in a broken home, children are reared in ways that are related to the existing model of what a family should be. The fatherless boy is not a child without a father; he is a boy from whose life a father is missing, although that father may be dead, away, or even unknown. All over the world societies have a vocabulary and observances to commemorate breaks in the biological family—words for widow, widower, and orphan, as well as, in some societies, for the man and woman who have lost a child and who, instead of being addressed as "Father and Mother of Someone," may be called "Father and Mother Bereft."

Everywhere in the world marriage signals the foundation of a family, as marriage includes the expectation that children will be born to the new couple. Yet everywhere some unions are barren. So every marriage also carries the possibility of incompleteness. Among the oldest tales and myths there are stories that tell of heroes and chiefs, kings and queens who have everything and still lack their heart's desire—a child. But people have dealt very differently with this central failure of expectation. In some societies the barren wife is returned to her family and must be replaced by a sister. In others, barrenness in a wife is a cause for breaking up the marriage. In others, a brother may give up one of his children to become the heir of his childless brother. In still other societies, as in our own, the custom of adoption allows a childless couple to take and rear as their own children whom others have begotten and borne. But everywhere life within a family is the recognized way for a child to be reared. Any other arrangement is a makeshift one, a misfortune for the child that he will bewail his life long.

Some peoples emphasize how much parents desire children. Others emphasize how much children need parents. The focus is on the family and ultimately on the individuals in particular families. But other peoples emphasize the need for children to ensure the survival of the whole group. Where this feeling of the community's need is strong, children are cared for and cherished by all the members of a clan or a little village; everyone willingly forgoes fresh coconuts so that the mother of a newborn child may have plenty of coconut milk, and the birth of a child may interrupt every activity— fishermen may pause in their work and farmers stay home from the fields.

In some societies the family is the path by which unborn spirits find a human habitation. In others, it is the path by which ancestors return to live another life on earth, and a mother may say to her fractious child, "The one reincarnated in you must have had a terrible temper!"

In modern industrial cities, men and women do not have children to keep alive the past or ensure the future. Their children do not kneel down to receive a grandparental blessing nor do they tend a shrine for their dead grandparents or more remote forebears. Individual men and women marry to enrich their lives now, and family life has its meaning almost completely in the present. Marriage and a family stand for a kind of human completeness and give individuals a sense of themselves as whole people. As ties to parents and grandparents, brothers and sisters, aunts, uncles, and cousins, nephews and nieces are weakened by distance, the little biological family becomes all important, the center of a complete set of shared hopes and fears. In every great city in the world one finds this emphasis on what children mean now to the parents who have the whole responsibility for rearing them. The less help the small family takes from relatives and neighbors, from public authorities and government, the more successful it is in the eyes of others. The independent family, living within its own four walls, self-sufficient and taking complete responsibility for its members in sickness and health, is the ideal family unit in the modern world.

In the past other kinds of families may have lived in their own single courtyard or in great compounds with two hundred or more other people. The married son's house may have been his father's gift, or it may have been built for him by his father's kin, or he may have built it with his own hands. A man may have had to serve for five years in the household of his father-in-law or a woman may have been the lifelong subordinate of her mother-in-law. The new family may have settled among kin on ancestral land, or the tiny family may have wandered alone, cut off from other companions for months at a time, with only a dog sledge and a set of hunting and fishing tools to ensure its survival. Yet all families have had—and have—the same basic tasks to fulfill.

In the family both a man and a woman find a physical mate and one person to whom what happens to the other is paramountly important, a companion, someone who is there, someone who need not be importuned and sought for. In the family a man begets and a woman bears children who are provided, through the care given them by both parents, with the human setting in which they can survive and grow and become full human beings. These are the only universal functions of the family. All others belong to some times and some places, but not to others.

A mother may take full care of her own children or she may share the task with other women—her own sisters, her husband's sisters, her husband's mother, or her husband's other wives, household servants or slaves, or neighbors. The family may take its pleasures together, as all of them together attend a feast or a fair, travel on a pilgrimage, or go on a camping trip. Or women may find most of their pleasure and gaiety in the company of other women, as men look to other men for companionship, and as adolescents seek for amusement together with other adolescents of the same sex. The whole family may eat three meals together or only one meal, or the women and children may eat in one place and the men in another. Cooking may be done once a week or five times a day.

These things not only vary from one society to another, they also change over time—who cooks and why; where and when the family bread is baked, at home once a week or daily in the village baker's communal oven; the kind of house a family lives in and the furniture in the house. Every time such a change takes place, people feel that something is happening to the family itself. And, of course, this is true. The adoption of a new style of housing, the disappearance or reappearance of gardens, the building of a local school or a centralized school, the substitution of lunch at a snack bar for the midday meal at home, the drafting of married men or the exclusion of married men from the draft, the payment of family benefits or old age benefits—all these things lead to small changes in the family form. And people tremble for the future.

But, in fact, the family is the oldest, most firmly grounded human institution. However great the changes may be in the proportion of the population that is married, in the age of marriage, or in the number of years people live within the family, whatever the size of the family may be, however much or little time members of a family may spend together, and whatever else they may do individually, apart from the others, still the family survives.

There are good reasons for the anxiety with which people respond to changes in the form of the family and for the enthusiasm with which reformers, prophets, dictators, and dreamers attack whatever form of the family is current. The family as a form is safe. But particular changes—changes that take country people into city tenements, immigrants across the seas, and young people to places where they lack the help traditionally given them by their elders—cause hardships, especially for those who are the pioneers in a new family form. They cannot fall back on the past and they cannot foresee what the new style of living may lead to. It may lead to new kinds of isolation; it may also open the doors to a greater opportunity.

Yet it remains the essential task of the family to rear children who can live out as adults a form of life they learned as children. Within the family children learn how, in their turn, to relate themselves to others, to work and play, make friends, marry, and rear children. Within the enveloping life of the family, each child learns who he is, what he is, and what he may become—what it is, in fact, to be a full human being.

In all old societies forms of behavior have been shaped through long centuries, so that they are adapted to both sexes and people of all ages. To be human, human beings need to learn a language, need a mother tongue. Once they have learned their mother tongue and, simultaneously, what speech is and what a particular kind of speech is, they can learn other languages as well. So it is with all that a child learns within the family. The family gives the child a name and a place, a home to which his right is unquestioned, a mother to comfort and care for him, and a father to lead him into manhood. In the home the child learns every fine detail of the several languages, in addition to speech itself, through which he can communicate with other people. Particularly, he learns to use his body—learns when to stand and when to sit; how to stand so as to show respect, courage, and dignity; how to enter and how to leave a place where other people are gathered; how to know that people are engaged in a conversation that is not meant for him; how to interrupt without arousing anger and how to take his leave courteously; when and how he may be playful; when he may lie down, alone and in the presence of other people.

Where there is a great diversity in the ways of different families, this too is prepared for as the child lives its first years in a palace or a hovel, with the whole family crowded into one room or in a house with a separate room for each child. From the first day when the newborn infant is laid down on a piece of bark or a soft cushion, is strapped on a cradle board or swaddled in tight swaddling bands, is tucked into the mother's kimono or into the hood of her parka, is fitted into a cloth swing or laid down in an old cradle or a dazzling new crib, he is learning who he is and who other people are. He is learning to live as a peasant, as a city child, as the child of fisher folk, or as the delicately nurtured heir of the rich and the powerful. He is learning what it is to be the eldest or the youngest, a favorite child or an unwished-for child. Most important of all, he is learning the difference between being a boy and a girl.

Whatever distinctions are made between men and women, elders and juniors, parents and children, the first born and the later born, the oldest child and the youngest, these are learned in the home, and when children leave their home they are prepared to find that others have learned the same things. In a very simple society, where all the houses are much alike, each house a child enters will resemble his own. If it is correct to stand below the ladder and call before entering, if small children are expected to go in and out through the back door, if it is polite to clamber into a neighbor's house when shouts or screams are heard, these rules will hold for one's own and for everyone else's home. If children are sent on errands that require tact or secrecy, he will have seen other children entering his own home as messengers and he will be sent to other houses. If his parents lower their voices in the presence of a stranger, he will learn the kinds of things that may—and that may not—be mentioned in front of an outsider. Whether a home is a place where visitors are welcomed or a retreat from which all men except his father, or all persons who are not kin, or all strangers are barred, he will learn this, and throughout his life he will be informed by this knowledge as he enters—or does not enter—the houses of relatives, age mates, friends, and outsiders.

In a highly diversified society, a child will learn to recognize the houses that are like his own, where he can expect familiar rules to apply, and those where he must pause to learn new rules or, recognizing that he does not know the rules, must be wary and watchful. He may learn that knowing how to behave in one home gives one a sure knowledge of how to behave in all homes, and he will grow up with a sense of freedom of movement. Or he may learn to have an anxious respect for the rank and touchiness of all who are different from himself and his parents. In his own home he acquires a model of the larger world, learns how people of both sexes, different ages, and different generations behave and how they treat one another. As he learns what a child can and cannot do, he learns what adults can do; as he learns what a boy is like, he learns also what a girl is like in his family's version of the wider world.

As each family also differs in some ways from all others, the child learns from the peculiarities of his own family what is customary and expected of certain families or all families. If most families have a cow and his family has none, he learns that poor families—or rich families, or the families of weavers or cobblers—do not keep cows. Whatever the peculiarity may be—the size of the yard or the height of the fence, having the only foreign-made car or no car at all—the explanations given him by his family as to why what they have is different, why they have one thing and not another, enlarge the child's picture of the wider world. From recurrent events and the facts of difference—meat on the table every day, only on holidays, or never, fish on Fridays or chicken on the Sabbath, or no meals during the day through the whole month of Ramadan—children learn the pattern of the days, the weeks, and the months for their own family and for other families. At the same time the child learns that families like his are many or few, belong to a proud, dominant group, or belong to an old and helpless or a new and arrogant minority.

As his home is one among many, everything the child learns about his own home also informs him about other homes on the same street, in the same town, in the same city, in books, in the stories his grandmother tells him, in the movies, and on television. "Once there was a beautiful princess who lived in a golden palace," the grandmother begins. "What's a palace?" "A wonderful, huge house, five times as high as this house, with wonderful rooms filled with treasures..." She herself has never seen a palace. She can only describe it as it was described to her, using as a measure the familiar things in their one-room rickety cabin through whose cracked walls the wind whistles.

As the child learns how its own home compares with other homes and finds out whether this is a matter for pride or humiliation, ambition or despair, he also learns that people who are like him and those who are most different from him all live in families. As he learns about variation and contrast, he also learns that other children—all other children except those who have been visited by terrible misfortune—have fathers and mothers, have (or might have had) brothers and sisters, have (or once had) two pairs of grandparents. Within the family the child learns about similarity as well as difference. He learns that all babies are born from a mother's body and that all babies must be fed; that men and women marry and bring up their children together; that children need the care of both parents; that brothers and sisters are different from friends and play-mates. He learns to see other people as men and women who are both like and different from his own parents. He discovers that his own parents were once children and that they will grow old and one day die. He learns about the span of life and the different emotions associated with death—resignation at the death of the very old, but heartbreak, despair, and an anxious searching for responsibility at the death of a child or the grown son or daughter of still living parents. Within his own family, the child learns about all families. As the pattern of male and female, parents and children, brothers and sisters takes shape, he acquires knowledge of what he is now, what he may be, what he can never be, what he can know in his own person and what he can only learn from others, how his life began and how it must someday end.

No one can learn to speak a language perfectly without listening to and talking with native speakers of every kind. And only by growing up from infancy in a family with a full complement of members will a child know the gossipy tones in which mother and grandmother talk together about midwifery, or recognize the bursts of laughter when father exchanges crude jokes with another man outside by the sheepfold. Too young to take in the full meaning of the words, the child grasps the tone—the intimacy in sorrow of women who are talking together about childbearing, pain, illness, and mourning; the intimacy in laughter of men who cloak many of the realities of life with protective humor; the special tone in which a father admonishes his son whose growth he both wishes and fears; the mixed anxiety and pride in a mother's voice as she acknowledges that her son is indeed a man in the making. As a spectator, as a listener, as a participant, the child has access to the whole gamut of emotion, both the feelings people freely express and those they seek to hide. Later, carrying in his mind remembered images, a man will guess at what his wife is thinking or feeling; responding still to old memories, a woman will guess at her husband's mood.

No one family is fully representative of what a family can be. The ideal family toward which every man aspires may be one in which at least three married brothers live in one court with their still vigorous parents and all their children. Perhaps only one family in a hundred will be part of such a large household. But children growing up in smaller households that only fragmentarily represent the ideal will still learn about the possibility, and the presence in their home of a widowed grandmother, a young unmarried uncle or aunt, or an orphaned cousin will give them some sense of the larger whole.

Where the ideal family is one with many children, people will commiserate with the only child, and his pleasure in being the sole possessor of his parents' love and attention will be tempered by his awareness of his isolated state. But where a large family means either continual or periodic deprivation—where no one ever has enough to eat or money enough for a special education—each child may daydream about the privileges and delights of being an only child.

The family that departs from the ideal no less than the family that best represents it carries the pattern for the next generation and sets its imprint of expectation on the growing children. What their parents have achieved, they may achieve; where their parents have failed in their realization of a good life, they may succeed. And even though the family pattern may be broken as a result of separation, divorce, death, or disaster, the child growing up in his family is given both an irrevocable sense of the individual's full humanity and a sense of the potentialities for depth and range in human relationships. A man may say, "My father had no education." In saying this, he not only acknowledges something his father lacked, but also affirms that he had a father. His statement may be a preface to his determination to be an educated father or to have an educated son.

Whatever his own family is like, the child learns what it means to be a boy or a girl, another person like or different from himself, what it means to be young and weak, growing and maturing, obedient and rebellious, possessive and generous, responsible and careless. He can see a plan, an idea that was conceived in hope while he was still a child, change its form and meaning as the whole family lives with it and slowly brings it to fruition, or he can see the effect on the whole family as one of its members relentlessly pursues an ambition or dreams a dream whose reality recedes with every passing year.

Because it is the family within which the child learns about his own and the world's potentialities, as they exist in the society into which he is born, all societies take extraordinary care to protect the arrangements that make it possible for each generation of young people to marry, for men to care for women and children, and for children to be born in wedlock. Rearing children in families does not mean that all adults must marry. But it does require a continual alertness to the conditions of stability, so that children will not be born and left to grow up without a family—parentless, motherless, or fatherless, and with no one to take the missing parents' place.

No society can protect all its children from the hazards of homes broken by the illness, insanity, or death of a parent, or from the miseries—and sometimes the tragedies—that threaten every member of a family when a very ill-matched pair attempt to stay together and rear the children they have brought into the world. No society can guarantee that every marriage will be successful, that all those who marry will have children, that all the children who are born will be well and strong and grow to productive adulthood, that a mother will not die in childbirth, that a father will not die of illness or in an accident. The conditions of life may be such that if children are to be fed and old people cared for, women must work outside their homes or men must go overseas to earn a living. A drought, a tidal wave, or an epidemic may fatally interrupt the life of every family in a whole community. Whatever safeguards a society builds into its way of life, it cannot altogether remove from human existence the element of the precarious.

But there are also preventable conditions that are not prevented. Mothers may die in childbirth for lack of care in a society that can afford to provide hospitals for everyone. Children may be born out of wedlock because girls are poorly protected or young men have no work. Where there are no remedies for the circumstances men feel are wrong, family misery is a measure of the poverty or desperation of a poor and isolated tribe or a struggling nation. But where families suffer from disasters that are preventable, this is a measure of a whole nation's neglect. A society imperils its own future when, out of negligence or contempt, it overlooks the need of children to be reared in a family—their own family or another one in which they will be given a sense of absolute belonging—or when, in the midst of plenty, some families cannot give their children adequate food and shelter, safe activity and rest, and an opportunity to grow into full adulthood as people who can care for and cherish other human beings like themselves.

The integrity of a society rests with the integrity of family life. This does not mean, however, that marriage need be the primary goal of all those reared in a family. Some children may, instead, look forward to devoting all their energies to writing or painting, teaching the young or caring for the sick, exploring the forgotten past or opening new paths into the future. Serene and happy children, children who do not need to spend their lives making up for defects in their upbringing, have the freedom to choose whether to found a family or to devote themselves fully to the kinds of activities that make high civilization possible.

When a people lives at the margin of existence, all adults must strain to reproduce themselves, lest indeed the people perish. But abundance makes possible a qualitative change. For now some members of a society may turn aside from their narrowly reproductive task and contribute to the future principally as the creators of ideas, as artists, and as the architects of new styles of living. Yet the transformation of a way of life and its fruition in creativity depend on the existence of a kind of family in which children are reared to perceive themselves and all others as full human beings and to see the wider significance each individual's gift may have for the world community. In this way change itself reaffirms the stability of the family's task.

IRAN

GREECE

ISRAEL

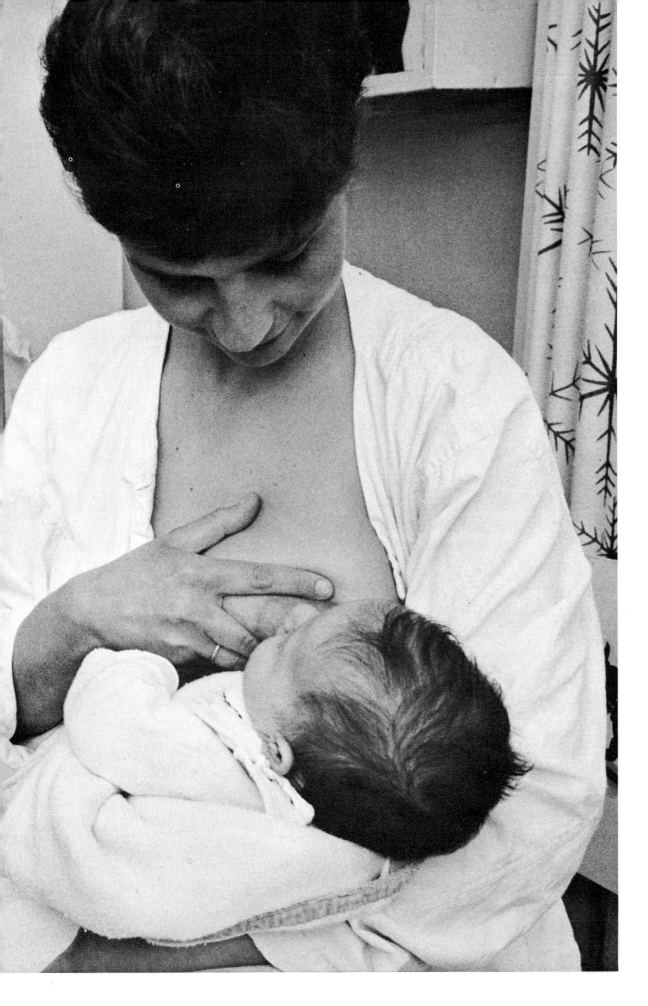

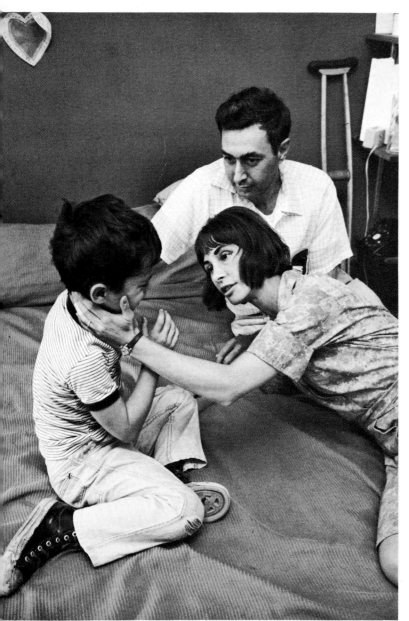

U.S.A.

90

FRANCE

U.S.S.R.

ITALY

94

HONG KONG

BROTHERS AND SISTERS

When a new baby is born, the world of the older child is enlarged but it no longer is his world exclusively. Generously or grudgingly, he must learn to share his mother's love and care, his father's games, his grandparents' indulgence, each cherished occasion— bedtime, waking to the sound of his mother's voice, the foam and splash of his bath— each delicious morsel of food, each plaything, and often the very clothes he wears. From his brothers and sisters, and the brothers and sisters he might have had, a child learns how to share.

This first experience of sharing is pictured in different ways. The emphasis may be on the child's feelings, as when someone exclaims, "Oh, now his nose is out of joint!" Or the child's position may be emphasized, as when he is called the "knee baby"—the displaced child who, still too young to run off and play as the "yard child" does, stands beside his mother while she holds the "lap baby" in her arms. But whether the older child welcomes the newcomer with excitement and hope—a hope that is somewhat dashed when he discovers that the infant can neither talk nor play with him—or greets the newcomer with resentment, as an intruder into paradise, he will henceforth see life with different eyes, and in the future his feelings toward all other children will be colored by this response to a younger brother or sister—welcoming or fearful, warm or coldly distant.

The arrival of another child also gives the older one his first experience of the inevitable. An only child realizes that his mother and father are very tall, but he has a sense of himself growing, getting taller with every day and gaining a year with every birthday. Not long ago he could only cry for the toy that was out of reach. Now he can take it down from the shelf. Someday the little boy will be a man; someday the little girl will be a woman. For the first child and for the only child who has not yet begun to think about brothers and sisters, the world becomes more livable as he grows and also a place on which he has imprinted his fantasies. Closing his eyes, he can wish his mother would go away forever; then, fearful that he may truly have banished her, he opens his eyes and finds her there, just where she has always been. He never entirely wanted her to go away, for his anger is weaker than his need of her. He can rejoice when his father leaves the house in the morning and throw a pebble after him to speed him on his way, but in the evening he will be standing by the gate where he can see down the road, waiting for his father's return.

But with the birth of the next child, the world is permanently changed. Wish as he may, the intruder will not disappear. He cannot be fed to the crocodiles, given back to the stork, carried away in the doctor's black bag, or replaced carefully in the row of cabbages from which, it was said, the baby came. The new baby is there to stay. Moreover, he himself has a new status, that of the oldest child, and nothing can change this. Not even death can alter the fact that he who was once his parents' only child is now their oldest child. The sex of the newcomer is also immutable. No dream can change the girl into a boy, the boy into a girl. And the fact that the newcomer is a boy, or a girl, both fixes and limits the sex of the older child. For now there are two—two boys, two girls, or a boy and a girl—and the sex of the one redefines the sex of the other.

This drama of the intruder on the undisputed realm of infancy is the most poignant the child will encounter, but as the family grows the oldest child must deal with fresh arrivals. The third child may strengthen his initial resentment and despair. Or he may now draw closer to his next younger brother or sister, and they may play in a world of their own making, apart from the mother who is busying herself with the newest baby.

Now there are two who can run away together and hide, wade in the brook, dig their toes into the wet sand, reach up for the fireflies that evade their fingers, or roll like happy puppies on the grass. Allied against the world of babyhood now occupied by another, these two gain a new sense of themselves in a children's world. In contrast to the newcomer who seems so small and weak, greedy and uncontrolled, they feel themselves to be strong and able, fleet of foot and sure of voice. The sense of companionship born of such an alliance never can be quite lost. Many years later, seeing a comrade fall in battle, the soldier who is left alive will be haunted by the image of his just younger brother, the boy with whom he shared his first adventures. Once a child has accepted a younger brother or sister, he will never again be entirely without peers—a child alone among elders, a child alone who can only wrap the covers over his frightened head.

Every child in a family learns different lessons. What these lessons are depends on the order in which the children come, which are boys and which are girls, how many months or years separate one from another, whether the next child is welcomed or lamented, and whether a child arrives in a time of prosperity or disaster. Many peoples recognize that position in the family makes an indelible mark on the child, and call their children First-born, Second-born, Third-born... Youngest. Sometimes these descriptive names are different for boys and for girls. When they are, the boy called Second-born Male is taught, unfailingly, by every voice he hears that he is the second-born son, something he will always be, all his life long. And the second-born daughter hears tales about other girls, second-born daughters like herself. Her mother says, "The first-born sits and eats her soup, but the second-born sits sulking and does nothing." As she listens, fear strikes at the heart of the little girl. Will she ever, ever catch up with her older sister? Will her hair ever be as long and silky, as crisp and curling, as live and bright? Or the younger sister may be the one who is taller and stronger, more skilled and more beautiful. The younger sister, recognizing what is expected of her, looks to her older sister in anxious emulation. But when she outshines her older sister, age is robbed of its reliability and the older child, sensing that things are not as they should be, feels shame. Perhaps what she has been told is not true—that to be older is to be taller, more skilled, and more beautiful. Perhaps, indeed, it would be better to return to babyhood, to be that infant, its every whim indulged, who now lies crowing and uncriticized on her mother's lap. Each failure, each unflattering comparison, each recognition of an inability to meet an occasion causes the older child to glance backward toward a younger childhood state only recently left behind in a proud effort to grow and be strong.

The recognition of differences in sex brings its own complications. In some societies boys and girls are treated differently from birth. Their names are different. A boy's name is a *boy's* name, a name that is never given to a girl. A different set of bracelets or a thread of a different color may be fastened around the girl's wrists or ankles. While the little girl is still tiny, she wriggles with delight at the sound of her father's voice greeting her as if she were already a budding woman. And the little boy blanches but draws himself up as he is greeted as a future fighter, a hunter, or a traveler in space. These greetings, so differently phrased, are remembered and compared, one with another, in memory.

The girl may become envious of the tone in which men speak to her brother, welcoming him to their midst and promising him by the challenge in their voices that someday he will go out to be a man among men. And the boy, listening to the softly flattering, cajoling, protective tones in which his sister is addressed, may come to recognize that she will never be challenged as he is challenged. She will not be asked to do things or to show what she can do. Simply by being herself she will win love. And he may envy her and wish that he, too, could be loved not for what he does but for what he is. But if his discontent does not blind him, it may in the end help him to understand the price his sister pays for the gentleness she evokes. He may more readily come to recognize that where he runs free, her steps are counted and she is held closer to home. And the girl, watching her brother, will learn that the price of being a man among men cannot be paid once and for all. A boy must strive unceasingly to excel. Over and over again, he must test his courage and measure his strength against other boys and, later, against other men. Very soon she discovers this is not her path. Following in her mother's footsteps, lifting her own small carrying bag to her head, carrying her first pot of water from the well, or hugging her doll, or a puppy, or the baby given into her charge, the little girl learns that for a woman being is more important than doing. She learns that one day she will have a baby, a child she herself has borne, and that this will be an achievement that is whole and complete, something no one can take from her and no one can diminish. If she realizes this as she walks behind her mother or as she stands quietly by while her brother scrambles up a tree or dives into the swirling river, she can be both content and impatient. And sometimes, caught by her impatience, she may look for half coconut shells and fasten them on her flat chest or disguise her hair, still cropped short like her brother's, with long locks fashioned from strands of grass.

Unlike the boy, who learns that he must go out into the world and make a place for himself by his own skill and bravery, the girl learns that her own body is the stage on which, first of all, she will act out her successes and her failures. Unlike the boy who flexes his arms and tenses the muscles with which he will tauten a bow string, wield an axe, rein in a horse, or brake a car, a girl may meditatively stroke her own skin as she wonders what kind of woman she will be and whether a child will ever stir in her.

In other societies no such sharp differences are made between boys and girls. In adulthood, each sex may keep to itself—the men sitting together in the street or in the teahouse, and the women confined behind high walls and latticed windows. But the small children run free and naked, their differences openly displayed and unremarked, leading to simple recognition without envy or undue pride. Girls and boys play the same games, sing the same songs, and learn the same lessons when they go to school. Their elders address them, all alike, simply as "child" or "children." Brothers and sisters have the same kinds of interests—listen to the same stories told night after night by the fireside, read the same books, or watch the same stories played out on television. They ride with the same heroes, galloping the same imagined horses to the same imagined victories, and journey on the same caravans to adventures in the same distant lands. Or they will play together all day by the river, making mud pies, and neither girls nor boys will define this as a girl's game.

Girls and boys, sisters and brothers, may live apart from the serious adult world in a children's world of play and school. Or girls as well as boys may spend most of their time with men, busying themselves with masculine activities and pastimes. Or the children may spend most of their time with women. Then the boys also will learn to care for babies and to cook, and they will go with their mothers and sisters to visit the newborn and mourn the dead. Later, all men will be left with a nostalgia for the childhood they shared with girls and women, but they will guard against it by renouncing all forms of tenderness, by speaking in loud, harsh voices, by making their stance aggressively masculine, and by exaggerating the heartiness of their relations to other men. Or women may be left hungry for activity, impatient at having to wait for men to take the initiative, restless when they are confined to their homes, and chafing against their feminine tasks of tending the hearth and caring for the children, sons and daughters who are already straining to go their own way. Or men and women alike, bound to the heavy routine drudgery of their everyday work, may look back all their lives to the lost freedom of their childhood, when no one held them back from exploring their own world.

In still other societies, boys and girls, brothers and sisters, learn that they are both alike and different from each other. They play together, but there is a boy's way and a girl's way of swimming and diving, a boy's way and a girl's way of running and throwing a ball. On birthdays or name days or festivals, boys are given tin soldiers and girls miniature dolls for their dolls' houses. In the temple, boys and girls have their paired tasks, dancing or serving or laying out the offering. Boys and girls are sent out together to gather kindling and pine cones, but the girls will search the woods for dry twigs and the boys will carry home the heavy loads. Or they will go fishing together, but the boys will cast the lines and the girls will bait the hooks and thread the fish on strings. Fishing may not be defined as men's work or as women's work, but as a kind of work that brothers and sisters, boys and girls, men and women do together.

In these societies, brothers and sisters are complementary to each other. However rivalrous they may be, neither boys nor girls shape their dreams by envy of the role that is not theirs. When they grow up, their long habit of doing different things together will make them into husbands and wives who can share each other's activities without feeling unmanned or unfeminine. And unlike men and women whose worlds are split by the very sharp differentiation of their roles, men can still look for companionship and friendship with women, and women with men.

However sex differences are patterned within the family, children must also learn to face the inexorable logic of elder and younger. Sometimes the elder child is classified with the parents. The younger sons remain at home, but the oldest son accompanies his father. Or the oldest daughter takes on womanly duties of caring for the younger children. If the oldest child's principal relationship is to one of the parents, he or she will experience the younger children almost from a parental point of view. Where this happens, brothers and sisters do not form a child society in which all of them are treated as essentially alike and different from the parents. Instead, they form a kind of ladder, each reaching up to the next older one for help and giving a helping hand to the next younger one. In a family of this kind, the youngest child is not striving and competitive, as he is in a family in which each child's task is to become strong and bright enough to share in the older children's play. Instead, the strength of the youngest child lies in his ability to demand care and indulgence from all his older sisters and brothers. And sometimes the older child, into whose care the younger one has been given, sees the parent as his own most serious rival for the little child's attention.

It makes a great difference within the family whether, when the third child is born, the eldest—the yard child—is granted freedom to wander away or, instead, must remain at home as the mother's helper in caring for the newcomer. Either boys or girls may be turned into nurses for their younger brothers and sisters, but the results are different for each of them. Where a boy is pressed into this task, he follows in his mother's footsteps, and later it may be difficult for him to shift to his paternal role. Where a girl helps to care for the babies, she is given a foretaste of her adult life; but where, instead, she is allowed to follow in her father's steps while the new baby is crying for care at home, she may become a woman who is endlessly impatient with the maternal tasks that bind her to her home.

In some societies, as soon as an infant is born, the next elder child is drastically weaned from dependence on the mother. However small and uncertain he may be, he is sent off, not as a nursling, but as the smallest and most helpless member of the children's play group. In many other societies, the infant and the knee baby stay close together and are cared for as a pair, while the oldest—the yard child—is sent off to join the children's group at play or at school. When this is done, each child, except the youngest, has the experience of being displaced by an intruder but has less experience of seeing the displacement of the intruder by still another child. The child's most abiding experience may be that of competition with the newcomer, and each child, as he turns to other companions, must always strive for first place. Where children do not come to realize the sequence of displacement as the common lot of infants moving toward childhood, they may become men and women who are forever jealous of place and position, forever fearful of being pushed aside.

In other societies, the family drama focuses on the three children at the bottom of the family. Where the yard child is kept close to its home as nurse for the newborn, she, or he, lives through an intense double experience, first of being displaced by the next younger child and then of seeing this intruder displaced by a still younger child who is, in fact, given to her, or him, as a nursling. In such a society, children experience a complete cycle of displacement and restitution, and this is sometimes also reflected in the rituals and theatricals that counterpoint the experiences of everyday life. In a society in which every child is continually enjoined to be gentle—first to the infant who has displaced him and then to the still younger infant given into his charge—adult dramas, enacted in the theater or portrayed in painting or sculpture, may be filled with complementary violence and activity. But in a society in which the older child is permitted to express vigorous rivalry with the mother for the newborn, dramatic performances may be exceedingly serene and placid; rivalry, given a voice in childhood, need not be expressed in the world of art.

Sometimes children are given names or are called by order-of-birth terms that group them into a set of four. This linking of four different brothers and sisters into a set imposes a common pattern on the way in which they—and their parents—look at life, for then the fifth child is not the youngest of the group, but, instead, is the first of another set. Or sometimes, fleetingly, in response to external circumstances, a depression or a war, the family is divided into two groups of children—the older ones who were born while the parents were young, and the younger child, or children, born at the very end of the mother's childbearing period. In a family of this kind the knowledge that one is a child of youth, with brothers and sisters young enough to be his own children, or a child of middle age, with brothers and sisters old enough to have been his parents, shapes the attitudes of all the children, producing a dreamlike overlap in their views of themselves, their parents, and the children they will someday have.

Inevitably, the first-born child differs from all the others. He alone enters the world as the third, breaking into his parents' relationship to each other. He is uniquely the child whom his father must learn to tolerate as a rival, and he can never, within the group of brothers and sisters, experience the position of a younger child. Each brother and sister who comes after him will for a time become the newborn center of the mother's care, but each, except the eldest, will also have to come to terms with an older child whom he has replaced, and each, except the youngest, will have to come to terms with the younger child who replaces him. Only the youngest is never displaced from his position of privilege. In this he, too, is unique. In some societies, it is not the eldest child who inherits. Like the younger children, he is given his portion of land or property and starts a household of his own. It is the youngest child who remains with his parents, cares for them in their old age, and inherits their house. There is, however, a great difference between the position of the eldest and that of the youngest as heir. When the eldest son is given all land, power, and authority, he must also assume some responsibility for each of his younger brothers and sisters; but when the youngest, the last and the least, is entitled to privilege and responsibility, he can always call on those older than himself for help. Elsewhere, the youngest child is never expected to take any responsibility. Unlike the older children, he remains dependent and demanding, someone who is always recognizable as a "youngest child" by his tone of imperious helplessness.

The relationships of two brothers, two sisters, and a brother and a sister are most sharply etched within the small family of parents and children, in which there is only one woman to hold a child on her lap or to mediate between two quarreling children and only one man to lift the child high or to go outdoors with the boys. When many relatives live as neighbors or within one household, or when servants or retainers form part of the household, each child may have someone to turn to—a grandmother, a widowed aunt, or a nurse—and someone whose favorite he can be. A household of this kind, with its complex patterning of trust, closeness, adaptation, and distance within and across generation lines, prepares the child, in his turn, to live within a large family. But the child who has competed for the attention of the parents in a small family, where no one shares their tasks, is prepared to look for the companionship of one person, a husband or a wife, whose attention will be undivided. In the small family, these two present a solid front against all intruders, initially even against the child who is born to enlarge the family circle.

These small nuclear families, consisting only of a father, a mother, and small children, are curiously shaped both to withstand and to fear change. Together, a cluster small enough to fit into a canoe, an ox cart, a small car, or the facing seats of an airplane, they can travel across the world, safe with one another. But the very completeness of the small family, parents and children who can pick up and go to the city, to another country overseas, means that the loss of one of its members will break the pattern forever.

In most societies there is a strong feeling that parents should not play favorites and every effort is made to disguise parental preferences. Where the eldest or the youngest is the heir, certain distinctions can be made in terms not of the individual child but of a special position. But in a few societies the natural tendency to respond differently to different children is faced and made much of. Each family is expected to have a "favorite" child, and a mother will look among her children to find one. And throughout the world, in the tales to which children listen, one of the recurrent themes is that of the child who does not belong to his parents. Perhaps this is an elfin child, changed in its cradle; perhaps the real parents deserted the child or are dead and these parents are really foster parents. The fair child of dark parents, the tall child of short parents, the one child who cannot sing, the one child with true pitch—such children will be singled out by their parents' wonder and the children in turn may wonder who they are and whence they came.

Yet the experience of having brothers and sisters, born of the same parents, sleeping under the same roof, eating at the same table, is an inescapable, delightful and repelling, desired and abhorred part of each child's life. In fact, few families ever fit the expected pattern. If the first-born should be a boy, the first-born is nevertheless very often a girl.

If sons are most desired, daughters are nevertheless born in large numbers. If it is essential for every boy to have a sister—for if he has none, whom will he exchange for a wife?—there will still be families without girls. And in some marriages, no child is born, in others only one, and in still others many are born but few survive. Styles of expectation also change as people change their mode of life—moving from the country to the city or from the city to the country—and as famine or war or depression threaten a people's security, and now as affluence opens new possibilities for care and education to large groups of people. And all men and women carry into their parenthood memories of their childhood relations to their brothers and sisters—how hard it was to be the oldest, how good it would have been to be the youngest, how dull it was just to have been the second or the next to the last.

Every child grows up in a world shaped both by his real brothers and sisters and also by his daydreams of brothers and sisters who do not exist. A deep friendship between brothers may lead both of them to expect that all other boys will be loyal friends. Or a dream of a brother may send a boy searching for so idealized a friend that none can ever be found. "I never had a brother" may be said with great relief or deep regret. When relatives live close together, the children of two sisters or of two brothers may be almost as close as brothers and sisters, and each child may find in a cousin or in a young uncle or aunt the brother or sister he lacks. But in the modern world, where relatives are scattered and each family lives alone within its own four walls, what one's actual brothers and sisters are like may shape the whole of one's life.

Within the small family, hereditary differences and the accidents of experience take on great importance. The girl who grows taller than her older brother, the younger brother who is stronger and tougher than the older one, the eldest child who is puny, the youngest child who towers over all the others, the girl who is fleet while her brother stumbles and falls, the boy whose skin is softer and more delicate than his sister's, the boy who prefers his mother's occupation to his father's, the girl who prefers books to babies—all these chances and mischances combine to shape boys' and girls' sense of themselves and each one's sense of what the other sex should be.

Twins dramatize for themselves and all other children the extraordinary fact of being born of the same parents. They may be identical twins—children of the same sex, each the mirror image of the other. They may be brother and sister, alike in everything except sex, so that each has a strange and special understanding of how the other feels. Or they may be as unlike each other as any other pair of children, yet be put into one pigeonhole by an accident of birth—dressed alike, when their preferences are different, and treated alike, when each one wants to be treated as a single, whole person. In the possibility of twinning, in the knowledge all children acquire that they might have had a twin, there is expressed the whole hope and the fear, the delight and the threat of having a brother or a sister, like or unlike oneself, to share every moment and thought and activity, doubling or dividing every pleasure. And herein lies the drama of growing up in a family.

Through brothers and sisters—those who are real, those who are longed for but never are born, and those who die or go away—each child is shaped and becomes an individual, different from every other individual, moving in his own way among his peers.

ISRAEL

INDONESIA

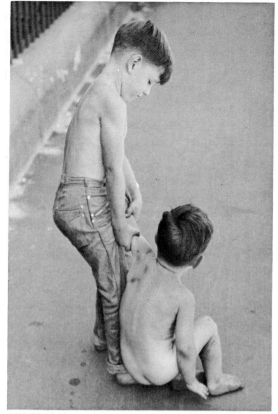

EL SALVADOR

AUSTRALIA

PAKISTAN

INDIA

HONG KONG

IRELAND

U.S.A.

HONDURAS U.S.A.

GHANA

U.S.A.

▼ U.S.

HONG KONG

▼ PERU

117

INDONESIA

U.S.A.

U.S.S.R.

GRANDPARENTS

Grandparents are given a second chance to enjoy parenthood with fewer of its tribulations and anxieties. Their children's children expand their vision of the future and at the same time are happy reminders that they have been successful in their life-task as parents and have brought their own children to maturity. Unlike the young mother whose hands are still tentative and uncertain, a grandmother lifts up the newborn child in hands that are experienced and sure. Unlike the young father who is caught by the demands of his work and torn between his will to succeed as a farmer or a hunter, a scholar or a businessman, and his desire to stay where he can enjoy his child, a grandfather, whose achievements are behind him, has time to tell stories, patience to teach familiar skills. Each new grandchild, each brood of grandchildren, can be a fresh delight, a deeply satisfying reward for the long years of parenthood.

For the grandchildren, grandparents are a refuge and a point of anchorage. The small child who, loving his parents, feels happy and safe at home may nevertheless fear that something might happen to his mother and father. If they comprise his whole world, it is hard for him to face this possibility of loss, however remote it may be. Grandparents whom he can visit, in whose homes he can stay, help to fill out his world and make it less precarious. They were parents when his father and mother were children, and now, long afterward, they are still living, active, and well.

Grandparents can tell their grandson about the years when his father was a little boy, as small and uncertain, as foolishly rash and brave as their grandson is and, like him, a boy who got into mischief, made mistakes, and suffered failures, the pain of which now has been transformed by sympathetic laughter. Grandparents can tell their granddaughter what mother was like as a little girl—a tomboy ready to climb trees or swim in the river with her brother; a quiet child who sat for hours sewing her doll's clothes; a curious child whose eyes and ears were alert to the nuances of adult preoccupations. Mother, who now is a model of propriety, is brought closer to her daughter as grandmother talks about her as a willful little girl. In her voice, as she recollects past misdeeds and the stance of a child stubbornly insistent on her own way, there is a mingling of old

121

exasperation, present amusement, and affection. And seen through grandfather's eyes, father does not loom so large. His booming voice and heavy, decided tread sometimes make a boy, for all his cocky bravado, feel very small. But as the boy listens to the bantering tone of the older man speaking to the younger one, he gains a different sense of the distance separating him from his father and from his own adult life.

Alliances with a grandfather are reassuring. In many societies where children are obliged to treat their father with the greatest respect, they are allowed to joke familiarly with their grandparents, pull the old man's beard, and laughingly call their grandfather's wife not grandmother but wife. The rivalry between father and son that once tormented grandfather and father is happily resolved as grandfather and grandson, joined in a playful alliance against the man who has replaced the one and will be replaced by the other, chuckle mischievously over their conspiracy.

From grandparents children learn to understand something about the reality of the world not only before they were born but also before their parents were born. "Through my grandfather, who knew his grandfather," a boy says, "I can reach out to things that happened a hundred years ago." Children can practice picturing a living world in which no one they know has played a part, and so they can also begin to think about a future world that stretches vividly—although it is as yet unknown—beyond the lives of the children they will someday have and the lives of their children's children. Experience of the past gives them the means of imagining the future.

From grandparents children learn about the whole cycle of life—what it is like to have grown children, to have lived a full life, to have completed the tasks one has set oneself, and to grow old. Old age seen only from a distance can be frightening. The bent and gnarled old woman who is nobody's grandmother and who lives all alone at the end of the village is often so strange that people think of her as a witch and point to her as someone to be feared, respected, and avoided at all cost. The irascible old man who carries a stick and keeps a fierce dog in his yard shouts at the children loitering at a safe distance from his shabby house. If he stumbles on the road, their fright may drive them to cruelty and attack. In a world in which the only old people known to children were lonely, strange old women and lonely, irascible old men, children would be fearful of growing old and fearful of what their hale and hearty parents would become as they grew old. The whole past would become something to be avoided.

But children can be rescued from a fear of old people by the presence of just one loved grandparent, great-aunt, or grandparent of a friend who is companionable with the very young. An indulgent grandmother who loves to have children sitting by her fire, gives them tasty food to eat, tells them stories, and shows them her treasures—her silver fan, postcards from faraway places, a troupe of tiny ivory elephants—listens to their adventures, and hides their small sins—one affectionate, familiar grandmother figure sheds a warm light on all the past and on the lives of all old people. And the touch of grandmother's hands, soft but wrinkled, skilled but trembling a little, tells children about old age long before they are ready to think and wonder about the meaning of getting old. Through a grandmother's voice and hands the end of life is known at the beginning.

Through grandparents children also can learn how their society keeps going, and what keeps it strong and steady generation after generation. For thousands of years a people were kept intact and alive by the strength of their social traditions. People had learned when to plant and how to plant, when to harvest and how to store the seed, what should be done at a birth or a marriage, how to deal with illness and death. Because the whole group knew these traditional things, they could work in step with one another. Without great uncertainty or bickering, the necessary things got done. The crops were planted and harvested. The fish were caught and smoked. The pots were shaped and baked, and did not crack when they were set on the fire. The annual ceremonies that linked the living and the dead, men and the gods, were performed. Every sound and smell was familiar. Every tool and weapon was known and its use understood. Change came so slowly that a man might be faced with only one innovation in his lifetime. In that slowly changing world, the grandparents' knowledge was a guarantee of steadiness and security. For the oldest people knew how the group had survived disaster, what they had done the year there was no harvest, how they had regathered their forces when the valley was devastated by an enemy raid, how they had buried the dead and cared for the orphans when half the village died of a strange disease. They treasured the remedies that might be needed only once in many years, the prayer for the rare occasion. From them young parents learned to care for their children as they had been cared for, and grandchildren learned how important it was to learn the old ways and the skills necessary to carry them out.

Until very recently most of the world's peoples lived a life of very slow change, but great uncertainty. They had no knowledge of how to prevent famines or floods or epidemics, but only the courage to endure them. Those peoples among whom grandparents played the most important roles kept to their old ways most tenaciously, even when their lives were shattered by change. Among North American Indians, where grandparents reared the children, people continued to speak their own tongue and remembered their past ways until the last old man and old woman died. Where a people's survival depended on the faithful observance of tried, familiar ways, grandparents set their stamp on those ways.

Grandparents told the tales of bravery, cunning, and daring. On their lips glorious deeds lived again as part of the mythology of the world's beginning. Generation after generation, they fired the imagination of children with stories of the gods and heroes who dared disaster to bring fire to the people, built an ark to keep the people safe, invented the bow and arrow, saw in the shape of a folded leaf the design of the first tipi, fought dragons, killed sea monsters, lived among the creatures of the jungle and learned their speech, led armies across the trackless waste, voyaged over unknown seas, protected the people, and gave them their precious and unique history.

In stable, almost unchanging societies, the old nurse and the child nurse adopted the grandparents' role, repeating the old ways faithfully as they taught the children the traditions they themselves were too ignorant or too young to modify. In more complex societies, where the children of the castle and the great house were cared for by peasant nurses, these women played much the same role that older women played in the village as guardians of the past who kept the growing children close to the earth and the fire, close to the old protective cautions and the old dreams. As grandparents provided continuity in simpler societies and in the isolated homesteads of colonists in new lands, the peasant nurse, the cook by the hearth, the groom in the stable, the shepherd, and the fisherman kept close to the past and close to the people the child who was destined to become a priest or a prince, a scholar, an artist, or a king's minister in some great city.

Today, in a time of world-wide, bewildering change, grandparents appear to have lost their traditional conserving role. All over the world young people are pressing toward new ways, pouring into the cities, shedding traditional garments and ways of behaving, substituting for them new clothes, new foods, new equipment, new furniture, new kinds of housing, and a new vocabulary related to new behavior. Alarmed by the overwhelming pressure for change, grandparents may raise an outcry against the new, and young people, fearing the counterpressures of the past, may feel that their only hope of success in making a new life depends on their leaving the village, the region, the tight caste-bound group, the little religious community, even the country of their birth, for some far-off place. Yet the security given them by their grandparents stands them in good stead when they have left their parents behind and, having broken their ties to the past, try to bring up their children in unaccustomed ways.

Sometimes the habit of moving as far away as possible from the old-fashioned grandparents will hold for several generations until, for a given family, the pace of change has slowed down. Then, as the gap between father and son, mother and daughter narrows, young parents find it easier to live closer to their parents with whom they once more share a familiar world. When this happens, grown sons and daughters have established their freedom to court mates of their own choice, make their own political decisions, seek a different religious faith, and bring up their children in modern ways—and grandparents have accepted the break with the traditional past.

In societies where these battles have been largely won, grandparents are acquiring a new role. Instead of being the most conservative, cautious members of the group, they represent through their own experience those who best understand change. Where they themselves have been the immigrants—the very people who moved from the country to the city, crossed the sea to a new country, went to school although no one of their ancestors had learned to read, became familiar travelers on trains and ships, in automobiles and airplanes, learned to use the telephone, listen to the radio, and enjoy television—they are the living proof that the human race is capable of changing rapidly and surviving intact.

A grandmother who started life wearing a grass skirt and who now wears a well-cut, modern dress and stands in line, wallet in hand, to pay her school tax, is a living refutation of the belief that individuals cannot reorganize their lives with sufficient speed to keep up with the accelerating pace of change. After the holocaust of World War II it was the old men in the devastated countries of Europe—the men who had lived through the extraordinary changes of more than half a century—who were able to lead, while their grandchildren were learning enough to become part of the new age into which they were born. Grandparents, who once were the conservators of the past for the future, now have become those who best know how to prepare their grandchildren for innovation and change.

Yet, essentially, their new role enables contemporary grandparents to carry out their age-old function of teaching their grandchildren how the whole of life is lived to its conclusion—in the past by running exactly the same course that one's father had run, and today by a readiness to run each day, each week, each year a new and untried course.

U.S.A.

JAPAN

126

PAKISTAN

127

YUGOSLAVIA

U.S.A.

PORTUGAL

129

VENEZUELA

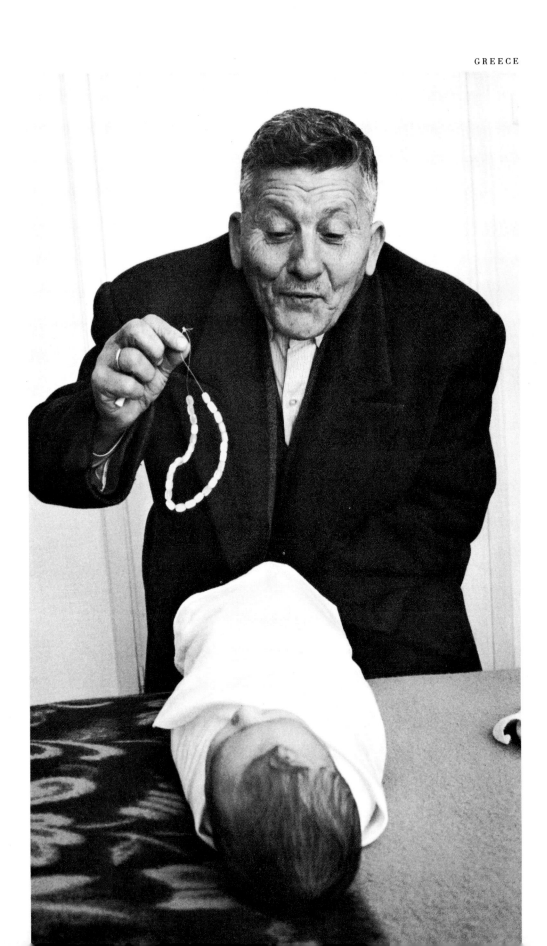

AUSTRIA

U.S.A.

COSTA RICA

COLOMBIA

133

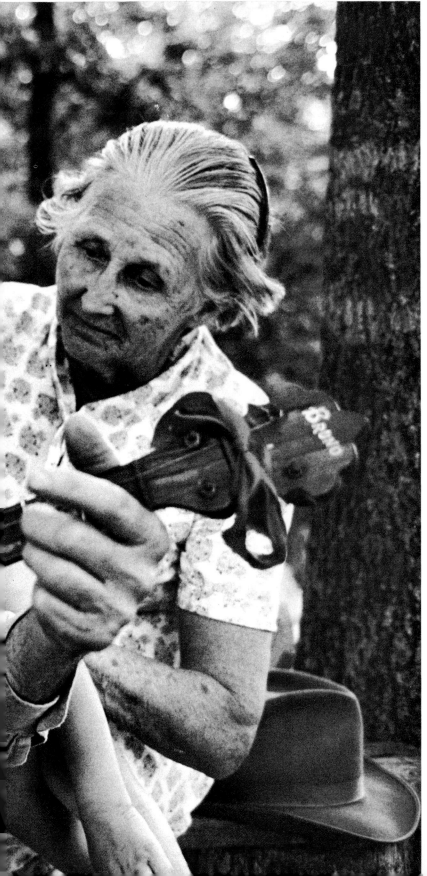

YUGOSLAVIA

ITALY

EGYPT

PORTUGAL

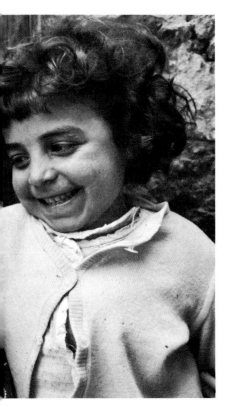

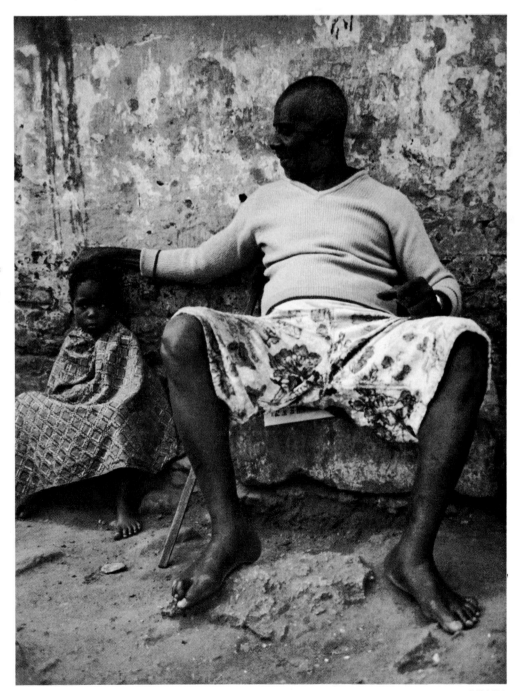

GHANA

SPAIN

THE CHILD ALONE

There was a child went forth every day,
And the first object he look'd upon, that object he became,
And that object became part of him for the day or a certain part of the day,
Or for many years or stretching cycles of years.

A child learns to be alone in his mother's arms. Held securely, warm and comfortably fed, he is content and his attention is free to wander over the surrounding world, at first fleetingly but soon with serious intent. For one child the sunlight dancing on the wall, the call of a bird, and the sound of falling water merge with the gentle strength of his mother's arms and the rhythm of his father's approaching step. A sound, a smell, a change in temperature with the opening of a door are the familiar heralds of someone's coming. And when the signs fail, when the smell of burning charcoal or boiling coffee, the creak of a closing window, the growl of the just-awakened dog bring no one, the child's eyes may sting with the salt of unrecognized tears. For another child this pleasure in things is very early detached from people and the world becomes delightful for itself. The flickering light has its own fascination. The child discovers his hands and spends hours interlacing his fingers, experimenting with the interlocking of touch and sight. Out of these early experiences, the child evolves a life style of response to the world and other human beings.

In cold countries and in countries where the seasons contrast sharply, temperature may be a continually intrusive sensation. Then, in later years, wherever a man may be and whatever he may be doing—looking out over the sunlit valleys from a mountain height or listening to the work of a new composer—he will have to stop and come to terms with the weather, the temperature of experience. Is he hot or cold? Or is he, in the phrasing of one language, in a state of not-hotness and not-coldness, consciously appreciating the perfect balance between his own skin and the surrounding temperature? In this responsiveness to temperature there is a continual play between the world within and the world outside the self—cold hands and the heat of the blazing fire, warm face and the brush of a cool wind. Each memory compounds these sensations, and later they are inextricably part of the remembered experience. It was piercingly cold. A fresh breeze rippled the water. It was a breathless night.

Taste and touch interweave with the sense of temperature—the taste of food coming to one only as an aromatic smell carried by the faint smoke of the cook fire across the courtyard; the taste of food that is hot and has a rough texture as it comes to one's lips; the taste of food that lingers after the spoon has been polished clean and the cool smoothness of the food itself no longer can be felt on the palate; the memory of a taste, an aroma, and a crisp crackling that is reawakened by the recognition of a familiar food or by the sudden awareness that this is not the same food at all.

As surely as each child responds to his mother's arms and voice and very soon to her face, and as surely as he learns that some people are familiar and others are strange, when he is about eight months old and "human beings appear in the pupils of his eyes," the child also learns to trust his senses or, less fortunate, learns that his senses may betray him. When the sound expected is the sound that comes, the child is freed to listen for new sounds. When the child has learned to connect and to hold the connection between the sudden quick gesture with which his Arctic mother pulls him out of her hood and the sudden impact of intense cold, he will no longer be startled by her gesture or the cold. When her gesture comes, he will brace himself in expectation of what will follow, taut but untearful, his attention already concentrated on the coming encounter. Once he has mastered this experience, he is free to try another. But the child who cannot be certain about the sequence of experiences—whether the cold will follow the swift, lifting gesture, whether a tinkling sound means the coming of warm milk, whether footsteps are approaching footsteps—will try over and over to master his sense of the world. This is the child who later demands the same walk, the same story, the same game day after day. And each time he is reliving a question: will it come out the way I think, the way I hope it will?

For small children in some societies the world is almost totally predictable. Every night a new spark lights the same fire. The cacophony of cocks crowing and dogs barking is the daily sound of the sun rising. The bird that is the second bird of dawn is always the same bird. Six days a week all women's clothes have the same coarse texture and on the seventh day they are smooth and silky. At mealtime the same smells float from every neighbor's house. The voices of the men shouting in the street and the voices of the women murmuring beside the hearth are related in their rhythms. Surprise, seldom encountered, is itself a surprise. The poetry the child learns is old, old poetry. People laugh at timeless jokes, and all babies drift into sleep with the same lullabies. Wind and snow, sun and rain, winter and summer, milk and spring water and wine come to him as familiar things that everyone knows, and his own expectations are colored by the feeling that everything has been and will be, over and over, the same. Still a child, his expression echoes the expressions of his elders.

For other children, reared differently, the patterning of experience is more complex. A child must discover continuity in change. Flattened against his mother's back, swinging in a cradle board hung from the pommel of a saddle, tightly swaddled and carried like a log of wood in his mother's arms, seated belted into the front of a car, the child experiences the world as a kaleidoscope of sounds and sights, caught briefly and lost again before they can be explored and fully sensed. Such a child learns to welcome and enjoy change. But he also may be overwhelmed by change that is too sudden or too great. The child whose mother's back slumps in weariness, whose father's voice snaps under the strain of driving on an icy road, whose mother is frightened by the strangers who stand, boldly staring, at the edge of the market, suddenly feels alone, lost in an alien world. For this child, for whom the expectation of change is touched by pain, strangeness may lose its savor. He becomes a traveler always seeking a point of rest.

The child's growing need to take in the world soon becomes as acute as hunger or thirst. Stars in the night sky, the waxing and waning moon, the earth's relation to the sun, the meaning of seeds growing into plants and plants in their turn producing seeds, the sound of nesting birds, the nuzzling movement of a day-old puppy, the wonders of different textures, smooth and rough, crisp and diaphanous, the precision of the instruments with which mother cooks and father works, the reliable and revealing sound of the car's motor, the jet stream that suddenly divides the blue sky—all these must be assimilated if the child is to become a person, a perceiving person in a perceptible world.

In some societies, in some parts of a society, or in some families, the child sees the world through the fine mesh of constructed beauty—architecture that frames all human movement, and poetry, painting, drama, and religious ritual that structure the experience of every human sense and emotion. The child sees the daylight as it is framed by a beautiful door, the natural world as it is captured in a formal garden. Food, subtly flavored, comes in a porcelain bowl, softly gleaming and shaped by a thousand years of craftsmanship. There is no way for the child to discover the moon. Moonlight glimmers in the figures of speech that tumble from his nurse's lips and the silver crescent moon is engraved on cup and plate.

There are children who flourish in a world where every image is foreordained. Their imagination flourishes and their appetite grows. Discovery is the uncovering of another whole world whose imagery also is fully patterned, reflexively shaped, formed, and polished by those who made that world. Growing up, they themselves will design other doorways, plant other gardens patterned on those they know, but still distinctive and beautiful. But for other children this fare is too rich. Feasting on it dulls their senses. In such an intricately patterned world, what pattern can they make? Rich fare stimulates some children. Others turn away from it, still hungry.

Yet unrevealing dullness is almost always more cruel.

A child can pattern his world with small things. Letting his eyes rove in a now-familiar room, a child suddenly catches a glimpse of unfamiliar color. On the paper label of a tin can the red gleam of an unbelievable tomato catches the child's attention. It is brighter, more wonderful than anything he has ever seen. In an ecstasy of delight, he searches for another bit of color, something else that glows with the same brilliance as that red. His eyes are awakened to color and he needs other colors to feed this new appetite. At that moment he is ready to match that red to the geranium on a neighbor's window-sill, the drop of blood on his mother's pricked finger, and the embroidered rosette on his grandmother's shawl. The rosette, the geranium, the drop of blood, the red tomato and, contrasting with all these, the blue bowl on the shelf, the blue tiles over the hearth, the flash of the blue jay in the orchard, and the faded blue of his own socks give him now, as his own possession, a world in which color expresses not a mood but a pattern of experience.

For another child, growing up in a drab room in a village in which every house is drably colorless, the red glow of the tin can's label will be all the more striking and remarkable. But he will find nothing else out of which he can form a pattern of colors. His thirst awakened and unslaked, he may spend the rest of his life thirsty and yet without any clue as to what he lacks or how he could quench his unsatisfied desire. Usually, however, he will resign himself to his familiar drab world. Only a slight melancholy will carry the burden of his first readiness to discover a world lighted by color, his eagerness to create a world that would reveal that flash of red and his enchanted response. A highly gifted child may experience such starvation of the senses and the mind as a challenge. Finally emerging from the dreary emptiness of his childhood, he may become a great artist or a great poet. But most children's imagination, given nothing on which to feed and grow, withers away.

It is the child's growing capacity to take in the world, rework experience, and give it out again in speech or song, craft or art, and in all the activities in which men engage, that is the source of individuality. It is the child's enjoyment of taking in and reshaping the world to a new vision that allows him to enjoy being alone. The child contentedly alone is a child becoming himself.

The child playing by the brook side, the child standing by the window watching raindrops splashing into a bright puddle, the infant crowing delightedly in the next room tempts the adult to reach out, interrupt, break into that solitude. Yet a world that is forever mediated by the insistent voices of other people is one in which individuality is inevitably blurred, in which no form can be freshly perceived, no discovery can be made, no reworking of a private experience can survive. A child needs a place and a time for experiences of his own if he is to cherish the world and blend his voice happily with other voices.

In every family, in every community, among people who are accustomed to the shepherd's or the fisherman's lonely life, and among people who are accustomed to the crowded loneliness of city streets, there is a kind of questioning about the child alone. A child is seen running over the grass, sitting by the water, peeping around a corner, leaning meditatively against a wall. Is this an aloneness in which the child is growing, counting over the delights of the past, or simply savoring present sights and sounds, looking toward the stars, following the flight of birds? Or is this child lost in loneliness, in need of a voice and succoring arms? Is the valley too deep, the wall too high? Or is this child who once discovered mountains in anthills now exulting in the knowledge that as his growth dwarfs old miniature landscapes he will find new mountains on earth and on the moon?

The desire to rescue lies close to instinct in all human beings, especially in those who once have been lonely children, for whom all isolation may be a burden too difficult to bear. For them the question of aloneness is always a poignant one, often a painful one. Is the child alone already resigned to hopeless waiting for someone to come? Or is that air of melancholy a first clear sensing that as the bright leaves fall, all things that are born must die?

Every child alone poses this problem for every adult, and all adults in protecting a child's imagination share, however briefly, the mother's problems as she tries to wean her child so that he will feel no sense of loss and will be strengthened by the comfort she once gave him as he now goes forth—alone.

JAPAN

KENYA

SPAIN

U. S. A.

PERU

U.S.A.

U.S.A.

NICARAGUA

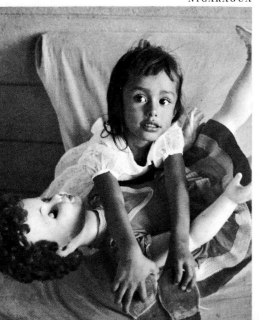

GHANA

ISRAEL

JAPAN

U.S.A.

160

U.S.A.

U.S.A.

HONG KONG

FRIENDS

There is a saying that God makes brothers but man makes friends.

Nowhere in the world does a single family, or even a large kin group, exist in complete isolation or make up a whole society. Even among the simplest food gatherers, where each family had to wander far afield in a very big territory to find food, there were other families. There have always been other families—families among whom young people have found their mates and families among whom they have found playmates and companions, trusted confidants and friends.

For many peoples, the family provided the pattern for both mates and friends. Sometimes two families that were related through a marriage would reaffirm the bond through the betrothal of a couple's children's children, and the grandchildren of this couple, in turn, would be betrothed. Over generations, in families that traced a biological relationship to each other, distant relatives became new kinds of relatives through a marriage, and cousins became the co-grandparents of a new generation of children. At the same time, men and women who were both cousins and brothers-in-law and sisters-in-law became friends. Where this was the accepted way, marriage and friendship alike depended on the fact that the partners—husband and wife, or two brothers-in-law who were friends—had not grown up in the same household among a group of children all of whom were preoccupied with the difficult problems of being older or younger, resembling father or mother, or receiving a greater or a lesser share of the love and approval of both parents. Children growing up in another family faced the same kinds of problems, but their loves and fears and rivalries centered on other individuals. However, the problems of the marriage partners were not diminished but intensified when, as in many societies, first cousins married and a girl's aunt became her mother-in-law or a boy's uncle became his father-in-law.

Tightly drawn family groups become deeply involved in their own internal loves and

165

hates. For a society to survive, there must be a broadening out of human relationships. Children must have opportunities to meet and play with other children, free of the barriers of too much knowledge mediated by adults. They must learn to know and trust others beyond the narrow family fold and beyond the small communities within which everyone is related through the marriage of cousins. They must be able to form broader alliances. Indeed, it may be said that civilization rests on the ability to make and keep friends outside the kin group and the group of those related through marriage, in a wider circle where friends can be chosen freely for their own sake. And the more complex a civilization becomes, the more emphasis will be placed on freely chosen associates, first as playmates and later as companions in study and work, as comrades in arms, and as political allies. The more widely the net of friendship can be cast, the better prepared each individual can be to create and live within a political community in which very large numbers of people feel secure and at home.

Among some very simple peoples who live by hunting and fishing, friendship may be the most precious heirloom that descends from father to son. As a father sees that his son is growing up, he takes the boy over his own "roads" and introduces him to the households of his inherited friends, and there within his own generation his son also finds friends. But just as in those situations in which cousins become brothers-in-law and friends, a network of inherited friendships allows for little choice. It is true, sons can let a friendship drop, but if they accept its possibilities, their friends, like their brothers and sisters, are the gift of their parents. There is always, of course, the openness of choice that comes with making a new friend. Two men may meet at a feast or they may fight side by side in a battle in which their tribes are temporary allies, and out of this chance association a new friendship may be formed. Often, where such a friendship is strong, it can be translated into a blood brotherhood in which the two unrelated men symbolically exchange their blood to form an irrevocable bond between them, a bond that may also bind their heirs.

In friendship as in love the jubilance of finding someone who seems to fulfill all one's hopes and longings carries with it wonder, a fear of loss, and a feeling of apprehension that this sudden depth of understanding, so different from the familiar understanding of close relatives, cannot after all be real or lasting. Tomorrow the companion will become a rival; tomorrow the friend who has shared everything in perfect harmony will begin to insist on always taking the lead or always following. Ranged against this apprehension are the formal affirmations of friendship—the children's pacts, the rites of blood brotherhood, the reunions of school friends and comrades, of men who have shared the same risks and hazards—the rituals through which new friendships are given support and old friendships are acknowledged to be unchanged. Human beings everywhere depend on ritual to maintain their firm faith in their own feeling. At the festivals that draw together a family or old friends, the lights and the food and the old songs reinstate feelings that may be wavering or uncertain. Yet it is the very freedom of friendship that gives it depth and meaning and poignancy.

Friendship depends fundamentally on a community of interest in the present, the future, or—most often—in the past. From the first friendship formed by two small children who dig side by side in a sandbox, not speaking but matching the downward strokes of their shovels to a common rhythm, to the well-worn friendship of two old men who sit silently drinking the last bottle of wine laid down by their regiment half a century earlier, it is this sense of a common interest that holds friends together. Initially, friends are chosen within the framework of some activity enjoyed in common. A friend is someone with whom one builds sand castles, goes swimming, ranges through the woods looking for nuts, plays checkers, collects stamps. A friend likes the same games, does things in the same way, follows the same rules. A friend does not ask to be spared, like a younger brother, or demand special privileges, like an older brother. He does not make winning easier, as when father pretends to wrestle or mother overlooks mistakes. Between friends there is no bribery.

A friend is essentially another person with capacities like one's own, who is interested in the same things and willingly shares the toys and tools and possessions necessary for the game. All family relationships—except the very special interdependence of identical twins—necessarily involve inequalities and differences. But the relationship of friends is intrinsically fair and equal. Neither feels stronger or more clever or more beautiful then the other. Sharing their interests they also share a common fate in the mothers who insist that the game be ended, in the teachers who ring the school bell that summons them in from their play, in the recognition of a lack of skill each would be ashamed to reveal to an older or a younger boy or girl, in their secret knowledge about the adult world. Friendship gives children a sense of themselves as individuals, not as mother's son or father's daughter, not as mother's daughter or father's son, not as the eldest or the middle or the youngest child, not as the brother who is taller or shorter than his sister, not as the protecting or the protected sister, but simply as a chosen companion. With their friends children are individuals in their own right, taken for what they are, loved for themselves alone, their strengths and weaknesses acknowledged and taken for granted.

Children and adults as well also form other kinds of friendships in which they seek to remodel the relationships they have grown up with in their family. A boy searches for more satisfactory brothers, a weaker brother who can be ordered about or a stronger brother who will take the lead, or a child searches for a substitute father or mother whose strengths can in some way make up for the defects of his own parents. Or children may seek out friends who will make up to them what they themselves lack. A homely girl attaches herself to a beautiful girl, a puny boy makes a hero of an oversized blustering companion. These friendships are common the world over, and the ties between pairs who choose each other out of loneliness, weakness, or despair can be very strong. But they are nevertheless compensatory relationships that derive from the weaknesses, the overemphases, or the unfortunate mischances within a family in which one sister is more beautiful, fragile, or homely than the others, or one small boy, more clumsy or more sharp-witted than the others, is left out of his brothers' and cousins' play. The custom of friendship makes it possible for anyone to right the balance that can never be perfectly achieved within the family—as it also makes it possible for an individual to rebuild, outside the family, the relationship to a lost brother or sister. But the intrinsic character of friendship is neither compensatory nor imitative. Instead it is based on the human search for symmetry, for a relationship of choice in which two people are equal and alike in all important ways.

Friendship with its symmetry is at the root of those tendencies that, with many different shades of meaning, we call democratic—the desire for others to have the same opportunities as oneself, and the demand that one be given the same treatment accorded others. No matter how angry a small boy may be when his elder brother is allowed to go fishing while he is kept at home, he realizes that, in fact, he is smaller and does not yet have the endurance or the skill his brother has. His cry is a cry of envy, and although he feels that his mother's refusal is unbearable he knows it is just. No matter how willingly an older brother pretends that his baby brother is a first-class opponent in a boxing match, he knows the disproportion in their strength and accepts as just his mother's refusal to let the match continue. Yet each boy keeps the desire for someone with whom he can play on equal terms, someone who is neither stronger nor weaker than he is himself, someone who knows as much as he does, but neither more nor less.

The realization of this desire opens up another world. The child reaches out for friends in other families, among the neighbors, among children whose families are richer or poorer than his own, who belong to different groups, look different, and arrange their lives in different ways. Finding a friend, he finds someone whose legs match his own in the sprint across the playground, whose eyes match his in keenness, whose laughter breaks out to match his own enjoyment of a joke, whose fury at an interruption of their play joins his in one cry of anger, and whose silence flows into his own. Friends who have discovered each other in play later will make common cause in their discovery of new activities and in their speculations. Together they will spend days and weeks taking apart and putting together an engine, building a telescope, making a mineral collection, reading about space exploration, daydreaming a career, each carrying the other into the excitement of a new pursuit, a new interest, a new effort to master the world of things. And those who have been joined in friendships of this kind will be prepared to work in and for a world in which there is equal opportunity in a sense that can never come about through the family alone, or a society that is modeled mainly on the family.

Such friendships, with their beginning in parallel play, sometimes are called mirror relationships, as each boy or girl seeks for himself or herself in the eyes of the other. But the image of the mirror overemphasizes the element of self-love and underestimates the element of trust. With a friend, with a group of friends, each dares to be himself at his best and at his worst. Each dares to share even the most craven fears and the wildest hopes. In a group of friends, the child learns to accept himself as he is and as he will be. And accepting himself, he trusts others with the same freedom.

In a group whose friendships are based on their common enjoyment of games of strength and skill, intellectual differences can be ignored. In a group whose friendships are built on the play of minds, differences in strength are irrelevant. Each child, as he bases his relationship to the others on something all of them can do, learns with their help to accept more easily the things he cannot do. Then, for that group, each difference becomes part of the whole. They do not value one another unconditionally, as a loving mother would, or aspiringly, as a father would, or with that mixture of love and regret brothers and sisters feel for one another. Instead, each is valued for himself, what he can do, and what he is.

As the world widens, friendship can include greater differences within its essential symmetry, differences of education, nationality, race, and sex, and boys and girls and men and women can find in each other both likeness and contrast.

U.S.A.

KENYA

JAPAN   ▼ U.S.

NIGERIA

U.S.A.

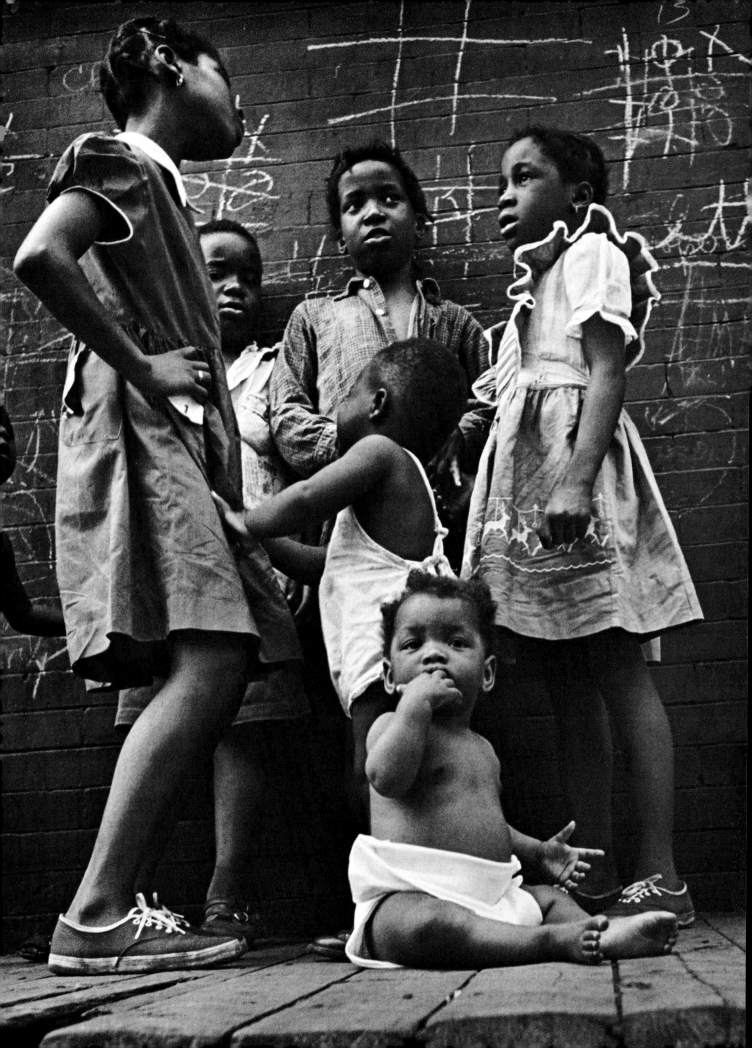

INDIA

EGYPT

JAPAN

U.S.A.

BRAZIL

U.S.A.

EL SALVADOR

MEXICO

COLOMBIA

178

GHANA

ENGLAND

NIGERIA

ADOLESCENTS

At adolescence children begin to move toward an unknown future. The translucent walls of childhood no longer close them in, for suddenly they discover the wide gateways and the gates ready to swing open at a touch of the hand. The way is open for them to move away from the family, away from the familiar gardens and ponds and woods where they came to know the natural world, away from the fireside stories told them by their grand-mothers, away from the brothers and sisters who will always be older and younger than they, and away from the playmates who shared their earliest games.

Up to adolescence the child lived in a circumscribed world. However individual and gifted, lively and intelligent he seemed to his parents, he was still a child for whom others had to plan, who had to be admonished, hedged about with protective rules, and kept within bounds. But with adolescence the old rules lose their meaning, and children begin to look beyond the old boundaries with new farseeing eyes. The adolescent boy gives up the dream of competition with his father in which he sometimes triumphed and sometimes despaired of ever accomplishing as much as his father had. Instead, he now looks forward to what he actually may become. The adolescent girl who once held her doll as her mother held her baby now looks forward in earnest, picturing the woman she will become and the living child she may rock in her arms. At adolescence, children stand at the gates, vividly seeing—and yet not seeing—the pathways of their own lives. For better or worse, each family has accomplished the task of caring for its sons and daughters, and they have learned, well or badly, the essential lessons their parents could teach them.

For the adolescent the paths leading out from the swinging gates are both entrancing and frightening. Even for the youth who has been an intrepid child traveler, the first journeys away from home may seem too difficult to accomplish. Girls who ranged the streams and mountains beside their brothers become shy and timid, their hands hot and cold, their smiles precarious. One day they want to dress as children, the next as women of the world. Each adolescent in his own way hesitates at the threshold. One sallies out and then, frightened by his own temerity, hurries back; but safely inside he looks out longingly, ready to be off again. Another hangs back, willing and unwilling, until at some sign known only to himself he moves ahead boldly, once and for all.

Everywhere in the world people mark the moment when a girl passes from childhood to physical maturity and the time when the boy's voice cracks and deepens and his beard, slight as it may be for some racial stocks, begins to grow. For the elders these changes signal the end of one kind of responsibility and the beginning of another more onerous one. Little children must be ceaselessly guarded and cared for, but adolescents, who still are in need of protection, are creatures whom it is almost impossible to protect. Their safety now depends on their earlier learning in childhood and on the way the other adolescents around them are growing toward adulthood.

In a society in which boys go out on dangerous raids, a mother may make magic to protect her adolescent son's life, but any attempt to keep him at home when others go out will also endanger him. Where adolescent girls have a special house to which boys come with flutes to court them, a father may tremble for his daughter's safety and fear that the wooing may go wrong, but by interfering he will only create new difficulties. In every society adolescents take over the world's ways and parents must yield their assent.

Sometimes parents are permitted to lock up their daughters, and girls can only whisper to their lovers through barred windows. Sometimes boys are shut up in schools where older boys teach and harry them and men wearing the masks of frightening authority give them a last set of admonitions about manliness. Sometimes, at the beginning of adolescence, boys are sent as war scouts on dangerous missions and on long night errands through the enemy-infested bush. And sometimes each boy must go out alone and wait, fasting and vigilant, in the hope of winning the protection of a guardian spirit. Whatever the customary ways are for children to emerge into youth, these indicate the kinds of paths adolescents must take. Individual families can neither shield their children nor safely direct them along different paths. Individual parents who set themselves against custom become involved in a much greater struggle than those who watch with bated breath as their children set out on their first adventures.

The world over, adolescence is the period of greatest differentiation between boys and girls, not only in the anxieties felt by their parents but also in the dreams that animate them. Yet the boy and the girl, each in a different way, are equally preoccupied by the task of becoming, physically, a man and a woman—no longer someone's child, but potentially the parent of a child. Within their own bodies changes are taking place that they cannot ignore, and in the world outside they are confronted by alterations in treatment that match their visible growth and approaching maturity.

In some societies adolescents are left to realize change at their own pace. No one records their age. No one complains about the slow pace of this boy or the fast pace of that girl in growing up. Children are safe in their childhood as long as they are unready;

and each chooses when to begin courtship and the first tentative search for a mate. One by one, the boys drift away from the boys' gang, take on the stance of young men, and move toward the girls who also, one by one, grow into readiness to receive them. No one will hurry them.

But in most societies adults express old fears and new fears, old hopes and new hopes as they urge on and hold back adolescent boys and girls, guard them and leave them to fend for themselves. All the girls may be betrothed early in childhood and sent to their prospective husbands' homes before they reach puberty. In this the girls have no choice. They must accept their new families as unquestioningly as they accepted the families into which they were born. And the boys, given their wives, have as little choice and yet are expected to be grateful to those who have made this provision for their future.

At the other extreme are the adolescents who are trapped in the neglect and poverty of great cities. Growing up in families whose kinship ties are disrupted and whose links to a more stable past are broken, they can expect no help from parents who do not understand their new urban life. Unschooled, unprotected, and unguided, each adolescent is left to follow the initiative of other adolescents. In a society that makes no coherent plan for them and coming from families who do not know what plans to make, they turn to radio and television, mass magazines and comic strips in search of guidance. Children of the mass media, they learn from headlines how other adolescents, equally at sea, dress and talk, think and act. In a simpler society, adolescents share the channeled dreams of all young people, and their parents, whose adolescence differed hardly at all from their own, can set up guideposts that will lead a new generation safely into adulthood. In contrast, modern adolescents are exposed to the fads and extreme actions of hundreds of thousands of young people who drift on a chartless course between a narrower, traditional world and a world whose dimensions are still unclear. All they have to follow are the published statistics of how many of them are now—this year, this month, this week— turning in questing masses first in one direction and then in another. For these adolescents, as in no other generation, the end of the journey in adulthood is unknown.

An unbridgeable gulf seems to separate the life of the five boys who are growing up in a shepherd hamlet, each of whom will choose a wife from among the six girls in that hamlet or the twenty girls living in nearby villages, from the life of young people who crowd, ten thousand strong, to welcome a television star at an airport. Yet the tasks confronting the shepherd boy are no different from those facing the teen-age city boy who moves so lightly to the rhythm set last week by a new hit record. For now, at adolescence, both boys must give up the dependence of childhood and move toward the autonomy and interdependence of adulthood.

Wherever a boy grows up, he must learn to leave home without fear, leaving behind him the old battles of childhood, and learn to return home from school or work or an assignment in a far city or overseas ready to treat his parents differently. Where he is permitted choice, he must be prepared to make a choice. Where no choice is open to him, the decision to go another way means that he must be prepared to blaze a new and lonely path. If he succeeds, he may open that path to others. If he fails, others coming after him may have a harder time.

For the young boy who rebels against the choices that have been made for him— refuses the wife who has been chosen in his name, deserts the craft to which he has been apprenticed, leaves the school or college to which he has been sent—the battle is a lonely one. At the moment of rebellion the battle is joined not with his whole society—for if it is, he becomes a criminal—but with his own parents whose demands he cannot meet. Such a battle generates an almost unbearable tension, as his old childish love and dependence must be opposed both to a desire for independence which his parents approve and to a course which they disapprove. In some societies, it is not only the rebel who suffers, but also the boy struggling to meet the demands made on him—to show bravery in battle, seek a vision on a mountainside, endure a period of poverty and self-discipline in a monastery, work as an ill-fed and much-abused apprentice, last out the hard grind before he can enter a profession, practice every day the difficult skills that will make him an athlete, a mountain guide, or a pilot. If he fails, or even thinks he has failed, he has been taught to feel he will betray his parents, and he may be tempted to revenge himself on them by killing the child they failed to rear in their image of what their child should be. In still other societies grandfathers stand behind the springing young boys, guarding their inexperience. But elsewhere there are no such safeguards. Fathers relinquish their authority early, and boys of thirteen or fourteen, long before they can break away in rebellion, are pushed into manhood and have the cares and responsibilities of manhood thrust on their shoulders.

The problems girls face, the world over, are not those that confront their brothers, but very different ones. For the adolescent girl may still feel like a child or she may still long to roam the hills with her brothers as she did when she was a child, but now, unlike a child, she can conceive. And long before she has the discretion or the judgment to choose among suitors or to weigh the temptation of the moment against her hopes for the future, her body, outstripping her imagination, or her imagination, outstripping her physical readiness, may involve her in an irrevocable act. The boy who breaks his bow string, turns tail in battle, hesitates before an order, or fails in school can still retrieve his losses by stringing the bow better, returning to school, learning to obey and to command. But for the girl herself and for society, the change is irreversible. It does not matter whether the child she has conceived is lost immediately after conception, whether it is born in wedlock or out of wedlock, whether it lives or dies. The event cannot be set aside. One more child, if it lives, will have started life in one way and not in another, and the girl herself can go on, but she cannot begin afresh.

Because parenthood for the girl and parenthood for the boy are fundamentally different, it has taken a very long time to develop contexts in which girls can be allowed to become persons before they become mothers. And because, in the end, the education of boys depends partly on the mothers who rear them, and the sisters with whom they play and compete or whom they cherish and protect, it also took a long time before boys were permitted to become full persons. Throughout human history, most peoples have been intent, most of the time, on turning most young boys and girls into parents whose primary task it has been to rear children who, in their turn, would become parents also. With rare exceptions, girls have always been reared to become parents, and persons only incidentally, and boys, too, have been reared to become parents, and persons only if they have belonged to some specially privileged elite.

But very slowly the burden has been lifting. Each small savage society had to lay on every able member the responsibility for reproduction first and then for continual, unremitting daily concern for food and for protection against cold and danger. The burden was lifted first from the sons of those of high rank and, occasionally, the youth of high promise, and later from a few daughters who shared, almost accidentally, in their brothers' privileges. Gradually it has been lifted also from larger and larger numbers of young people in those countries that have conquered the relentless problems of hunger and cold. In the past, most boys, as soon as they left childhood, had no choice but to hunt, herd sheep, fish, toil in the fields, or work at a craft, or, in more recent times, work as unskilled laborers who never earned more than was enough to buy tomorrow's food and pay next week's rent. But in modern societies, it has been possible to keep an ever larger number of adolescents in school and to give them an opportunity to think further than their fathers thought, explore the life of other periods and other cultures, and to become both civilized men, inheritors of the past, and modern men, ready to make a different future. And as our capacity to free more adolescents has increased, our willingness also has grown to permit them to become what they have the potentiality to be as persons.

This change has coincided with a tremendous increase in the world's population. In the past, men struggled desperately to preserve the small tribes or nations to which they owed their sense of identity. Today we are engaged in a common enterprise in the attempt to preserve mankind, as all men are endangered by the weapons of destruction they have now—and will always have—the knowledge to build. In the past people counted the children who were born, wept for the many who died, and wondered whether the living were enough to do the work, guard the group from danger, and reproduce the group in the next generation. Now we know we must stem the uncontrolled growth of the earth's population. When almost all children live, fewer children need be born. When almost no mothers die, fewer women need bear children. When as many children grow up in small families as once survived only in very large families, so many of whose children died, men and women need not marry so early or devote so large a part of their lives to parenthood. Now, when our task is to balance the world's population at a level at which every child who is born anywhere, in the most remote valley and on the highest plateau, will have an opportunity to become a person, we do not need to organize the world in such a way that the relentless, unremitting needs of parenthood and poverty weigh down adolescents as soon as they leave childhood behind, making them old before their time. Our new command of nature, which makes it possible for the first time in human history to organize a world without war, save the children who are born, and feed and clothe every child, also allows us to offer to all adolescents, not only the chosen and privileged few, a chance to grow further.

Man's history has been one of longer and longer periods of growth. In the very distant past, before men as we know them had evolved, the period of growth must have been even shorter and boys must have been ready for the tasks of procreation and parenthood very young. Later, when members of our own species were living under extremely primitive conditions, boys had learned all they needed to know in order to survive by the time they were six or seven years of age, but they matured more slowly. At adolescence they were ready to assume the responsibilities of manhood, and so it has remained for primitive men, for peasants, and for the poor in industrial cities. The demands made on them permitted them to grow no more. Even when the years of education lengthened a little in the more fortunate modern countries, the idea survived that growth stopped somewhere in mid-adolescence. There was, as there still is, a general expectation that most young people would give up learning and growing when they left school. Set in a mold, they were ready to work day in and day out, because otherwise they and their children would not eat. They stepped from childhood to adolescence and from early adolescence immediately into maturity, and then aged early.

But in the last ten thousand years—and possibly for a longer time—some societies began to benefit from the accumulated knowledge that made it possible for men to plan ahead—to raise more food than they immediately needed, to store food, and to feed a larger number of people—so that some men were freed to study, to think, and to build a larger tradition. In time, in some societies, men watched the stars and measured the phases of the sun and the moon, designed great buildings, carved, painted, created systems of notation, built cities and organized nations, and dreamed of including all men, not merely the members of their own tribe, their own city, or their own race, within one system of values, cherishing common goals.

With leisure and the freedom given to some young men to pursue the new arts and sciences of civilization, a new human capacity was discovered: the idealism of adolescence. Among a primitive people, as each new generation lives much the same life the parent generation also lived, adolescents do not reveal their capacity to dream soaring dreams, make mighty plans, leap in thought to new formulations of the relations of mind and matter, and visualize the place of man on earth, in the solar system, in the galaxy, in an expanding universe. Until men lived in the kinds of societies in which leisure was a possibility, and a few adolescents had time to grow further away from childhood, youth was untouched by idealism. Indeed, in many societies, young people were more cowed, more submissive, and less rebellious than their aging and less responsible elders.

With the development of civilization, as knowledge accumulated and systems of writing made it possible to preserve and communicate to others, as yet unborn, what was known, new processes of development were also revealed in adolescents. Moving away from childhood, boys and young men were no longer exposed only to the drudgery and the small excitements of the daily round. Some of them, at least, heard and saw and read about the things earlier great men had dreamed of and sung of, written about, and built. The spacious vision of the exceptional man did not die with him, but became the property of young men who came after him. In each generation there were young men, and occasionally young women, who could match the unsatisfactory present against the prophecies of a better future or the dream of a golden past, and these young people, in their turn, were led to prophesy, strike out in bold adventure, break the bonds of tradition, discover new fields, and plunge forward into some new understanding of the universe and man.

In any growing civilization, some young men have been allowed to live out and prolong their adolescence, free from the pressure to marry and from the necessity of working for their bread. This leisure not only has given them time to grow, but also time for friendship before parenthood. It is essentially in the continuation of companionship outside the family, in relationships other than those concerned with courtship, marriage, and parenthood, that adolescents can seek and find the strength and the vision to carry one step farther the civilization into which they were born and of which they are the heirs. The urgent desire, everywhere in the world, to give children more schooling and more time to learn has at its base a very profound need. The rationale of educational plans in the contemporary world is the necessity of having a more literate population, able to do the work of a more literate and complicated society. But the underlying need goes far beyond this. Giving children time to prolong their growing is intrinsic to the very creation of that literate and complicated society. Without vision the people perish, and the power of seeing visions must be fostered in adolescents if we are to have the visionaries the world needs.

For many centuries civilizations have struggled with the problem of how to give men—and sometimes women—the freedom in which inspiration, knowledge, and art can flower. One solution has been to create a dichotomy in which the life of sex and parenthood has been set apart from a life of celibacy, asceticism, and thought or prayer. In a society that accepted this solution, the parent was never so specialized or developed a person as were those who carried on the spiritual, intellectual, and artistic work of the world. Moreover, every child was presented with two conflicting life paths, as he had to choose between the pursuit of knowledge, on the one hand, and the life of the family, on the other. Only in the next generation, if he chose to have children, might a son realize his other dreams and, turning away from parenthood, devote himself entirely to religion, the arts, scholarship, or science. In other societies, all boys have lived for a period apart from the secular world, as a way of giving them access to traditional knowledge and insight into the spiritual resources of a great religion, as one aspect of their on-going lives. In still other societies, childhood and old age were equated in the sense that the intensive learning of childhood, practiced throughout life, came to flower only when men retired from everyday responsibilities and could devote themselves wholly to thought, poetry, painting, and music. But all these have been essentially conservative solutions, the solutions worked out by societies among whom only a few were the chosen carriers of a great tradition, and only a few had the freedom to become creative individuals.

In most modern societies this selection and segregation of the few from the many is breaking down. Those who dedicate themselves wholly to important work now live in the world. Even though they may not marry, they do not live a life apart. However, where once the population was divided into the many who bore and reared children and the few who had time all their lives to think and to grow, there is now developing in many parts of the modern world a new dichotomy based on sex. For increasingly, adolescent boys are being educated, while girls, like the vast majority of men and women in medieval Europe who chose parenthood, are asked to set aside their dreams of what they might become in favor of immediate marriage and parenthood.

In creating this new dichotomy we resemble the primitive peoples who did not understand paternity. For we do not take into account fatherhood or realize that in establishing a kind of society in which girls must become mothers as adolescents, before they have had time to become individuals, we also are forcing boys to become fathers before they have become individuals. In our civilization we are the beneficiaries of poor societies in which only a few had leisure, but we are not yet fully conscious of the power our new affluence gives us to make all men the beneficiaries of that past and to open the way for every adolescent to grow slowly through a long youth into mature individuality.

All around the world, youth is stirring. Often that stirring is the blind movement of disorganized mobs. There is a restlessness that is widely expressed in demands for privilege, for power, for change, for marriage as a right rather than as a responsibility, and for parenthood as a pleasure rather than as a vocation. That blind movement and those demands express the deep contradictions characteristic of our time—a time of transition.

Perhaps even more important than the revolution in the lives of peoples who for centuries have been subjected to tyranny and alien authority is the surging revolution of young people who are seeking a new place in a new kind of world. The more rapidly the world changes, the greater is the contrast between older people, who have had to learn so many new things during their lifetime, and younger people, who take the same things for granted. Young people who all their lives have been familiar with cars and how they are driven, who know how a jet plane is operated and how a computer is built, have an appearance of startling precocity as they move among adults for whom this knowledge and these skills are still new and strange. How can parents feel that their adolescent children are, in fact, adolescents, when these children know so much that they, the parents, learned only yesterday and with great difficulty? The authority in adult voices flickers, hesitates, grows shrill, and young people, sensing adult uncertainty and weakness, press harder against the barriers that hold them back from full participation in life. From their viewpoint they are asking for full citizenship and the right to be men and women at once, because they are already more skilled and knowledgeable than their parents. But the fulfillment of their demands would have the effect of putting the clock back, rather than moving it forward, and of reinstating a kind of world in which all young people were set to work at sober, confining tasks as soon as they were able to undertake them. At the threshold of a new age, it is as if a generation was turning in blind flight from its vast possibilities.

For all over the world a new age is struggling to be born, an age in which all children can grow up in families and all adolescents can have time to become individuals who are able to meet the demands of a fully adult life. In this new age, in which adolescents need not be forced to become mothers and fathers and grow old before their time, we can set a new value on adolescence of the mind and the spirit. In a society in which no one will be forced into premature adulthood, many people will remain adolescents all their lives, following a vision that is not yet clear, puzzling over a theory that is not yet fully formulated, attempting to create in sound or in color, in meditation or in prayer, in the laboratory or in the library, in the halls of government or in the councils of the nations something as yet unknown.

For long ages the prospect opening out from childhood closed in almost at once. Only a few were free long enough to glimpse a wider horizon, a visionary gleam. With the knowledge gained through their labor and their imagination, still more could be set free. When childhood stretched only a few years ahead, early man was set free to learn a little; when adolescence was prolonged, the men of earlier civilizations were able to leap ahead. In the future we may hope to meet the magnificent responsibilities of our knowledge through the visions of boys and girls who will remain all their lives, not only as adolescents but as adults, open to the widest prospects, "moving about in worlds not realized."

U.S.S.R.

NIGERIA

INDONESIA

FRANCE

THAILAND

MEXICO

U.S.A.

HOLLAND

PUERTO RICO

NIGERIA

COLOMBIA

201

NIGERIA

CANADA

INDONESIA

U.S.A.   ▼ U.S.A.   COLOMBIA

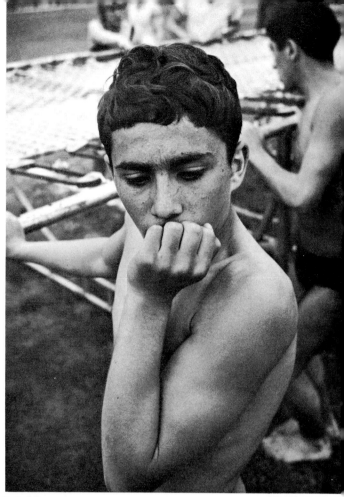

INDIA ▼ U.S.A. U.S.S.R. ▼ NIGERIA

ENGLAND